GW00792479

This revision guide is matched to the new single award OCR GCSE Science B specification (J640), from the Gateway Science Suite. As such, it provides full coverage of the Key Stage 4 Programme of Study for Science.

The guide is designed to reflect the structure and ethos of the specification; it focuses on scientific explanations, theories and models, and explores the impact of science on society.

As a revision guide, this book focuses on the material on which you will be tested in the exams and covers the content of the six modules: Biology 1, Chemistry 1, Physics 1, Biology 2, Chemistry 2 and Physics 2.

You will have to sit two exams. An overview is provided below, with details of where the relevant material can be found in this guide:

Although it does not directly cover the Skills Assessment ('Can Do' tasks and report on Science in the News), which is marked by your science teacher(s), the information provided in this guide should help you to complete these activities.

The contents list and page headers in this guide clearly identify the separate modules, to help you revise for each paper individually, and the pages are colour-coded so that you can easily distinguish between biology (green), chemistry (orange) and physics (blue).

> **HT** This guide can be used to revise for both the Foundation and Higher Tier exam papers. Content that will only be tested on the Higher Tier papers appears in a coloured box, and can be easily identified by the symbol **HT**.

You will find a glossary at the back, providing clear definitions of key words and phrases, and there is a copy of the periodic table for reference overleaf.

Don't just read the guide – learn activel will help you to remember, no matter how trivial it may seem, and constantly test yourself without looking at the text.

Good luck with your exams!

Authors: Jacqueline Punter (Biology) is an expert in biochemistry who has taught biology at Key Stages 4 and 5 for over 17 years. She also taught Health and Social Care and has an excellent understanding of the practical applications of science and their impact on society.

Steve Langfield (Chemistry) has been a science teacher for over 20 years and is an experienced examiner and moderator. He currently works as a science coordinator at a designated Specialist Science School, at the forefront of innovation in science and mathematics.

Robert Johnson (Physics) is a full-time teacher of physics and housemaster at a respected co-educational public school. He has an innovative approach towards teaching, which makes physics – sometimes considered a dry and dull subject – relevant and interesting.

Project Editor: Rachael Hemsley
Editor: Rebecca Skinner
Cover and concept design: Sarah Duxbury
Designer: Richard Arundale

ISBN 1-905129-61-0

Published by Lonsdale, a division of Huveaux Plc.

Title	What is Being Assessed?	Duration	Weighting	Total Mark	Page Numbers
Unit 1	Modules B1, C1 and P1	1 hour	33.3%	60	Pages 4–55
Unit 2	Modules B2, C2 and P2	1 hour	33.3%	60	Pages 56–102

Periodic Table

Key

Mass number →

1
H
hydrogen
1

Atomic number (Proton number) →

Main table (mass number, symbol, name, atomic number)

1	2											3	4	5	6	7	8 or 0
																	4 **He** helium 2
7 **Li** lithium 3	9 **Be** beryllium 4											11 **B** boron 5	12 **C** carbon 6	14 **N** nitrogen 7	16 **O** oxygen 8	19 **F** fluorine 9	20 **Ne** neon 10
23 **Na** sodium 11	24 **Mg** magnesium 12											27 **Al** aluminium 13	28 **Si** silicon 14	31 **P** phosphorus 15	32 **S** sulphur 16	35 **Cl** chlorine 17	40 **Ar** argon 18
39 **K** potassium 19	40 **Ca** calcium 20	45 **Sc** scandium 21	48 **Ti** titanium 22	51 **V** vanadium 23	52 **Cr** chromium 24	55 **Mn** manganese 25	56 **Fe** iron 26	59 **Co** cobalt 27	59 **Ni** nickel 28	63 **Cu** copper 29	64 **Zn** zinc 30	70 **Ga** gallium 31	73 **Ge** germanium 32	75 **As** arsenic 33	79 **Se** selenium 34	80 **Br** bromine 35	84 **Kr** krypton 36
85 **Rb** rubidium 37	88 **Sr** strontium 38	89 **Y** yttrium 39	91 **Zr** zirconium 40	93 **Nb** niobium 41	96 **Mo** molybdenum 42	98 **Tc** technetium 43	101 **Ru** ruthenium 44	103 **Rh** rhodium 45	106 **Pd** palladium 46	108 **Ag** silver 47	112 **Cd** cadmium 48	115 **In** indium 49	119 **Sn** tin 50	122 **Sb** antimony 51	128 **Te** tellurium 52	127 **I** iodine 53	131 **Xe** xenon 54
133 **Cs** caesium 55	137 **Ba** barium 56	139 **La** lanthanum 57	178 **Hf** hafnium 72	181 **Ta** tantalum 73	184 **W** tungsten 74	186 **Re** rhenium 75	190 **Os** osmium 76	192 **Ir** iridium 77	195 **Pt** platinum 78	197 **Au** gold 79	201 **Hg** mercury 80	204 **Tl** thallium 81	207 **Pb** lead 82	209 **Bi** bismuth 83	210 **Po** polonium 84	210 **At** astatine 85	222 **Rn** radon 86
223 **Fr** francium 87	226 **Ra** radium 88	227 **Ac** actinium 89															

Lanthanides

140 **Ce** cerium 58	141 **Pr** praseodymium 59	144 **Nd** neodymium 60	147 **Pm** promethium 61	150 **Sm** samarium 62	152 **Eu** europium 63	157 **Gd** gadolinium 64	159 **Tb** terbium 65	162 **Dy** dysprosium 66	165 **Ho** holmium 67	167 **Er** erbium 68	169 **Tm** thulium 69	173 **Yb** ytterbium 70	175 **Lu** lutetium 71

Actinides

232 **Th** thorium 90	231 **Pa** protactinium 91	238 **U** uranium 92	237 **Np** neptunium 93	242 **Pu** plutonium 94	243 **Am** americium 95	247 **Cm** curium 96	247 **Bk** berkelium 97	251 **Cf** californium 98	254 **Es** einsteinium 99	253 **Fm** fermium 100	256 **Md** mendelevium 101	254 **No** nobelium 102	257 **Lw** lawrencium 103

→ The columns of elements going down are called groups.

→ The lines of elements going across are called periods.

Contents

Fit for Life

Health and Fitness

Health and fitness refer to a person's physical wellbeing. Being healthy means being free from infection (no coughs, colds or diseases), and being fit relates to how much physical activity you are capable of doing and how quickly your body recovers afterwards.

Different types of exercise develop different aspects of fitness, which are all measurable, for example:

- strength
- stamina
- flexibility
- agility
- speed.

Cardiovascular efficiency – how well the heart copes with aerobic exercise and how quickly it recovers afterwards – is often used as a measure of general fitness.

The Circulatory System

The **heart** pumps blood around the body in **blood vessels** called **arteries**, **capillaries** and **veins**. It beats automatically but the rate varies depending on the body's level of stress and exertion.

The heart is a **muscular** pump. It alternately relaxes to fill with blood and contracts to squeeze the blood out into the arteries, so the blood is always under **pressure**. This ensures that it reaches all the cells to supply them with oxygen and glucose for respiration (see p.5).

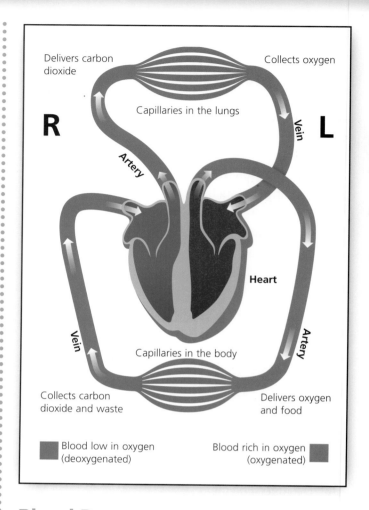

R / L

Delivers carbon dioxide

Collects oxygen

Capillaries in the lungs

Vein

Artery

Heart

Vein

Artery

Capillaries in the body

Collects carbon dioxide and waste

Delivers oxygen and food

Blood low in oxygen (deoxygenated)

Blood rich in oxygen (oxygenated)

Blood Pressure

Blood pressure is a measure of **the force of blood per unit area** as it flows through the arteries. It is measured in mm Hg (millimetres of mercury).

Blood pressure is at its highest when the heart muscle contracts, forcing blood into the arteries. This is called the **systolic blood pressure**. When the heart relaxes, the pressure in the arteries drops. This is called the **diastolic blood pressure**.

Healthy Blood Pressure

Normal blood pressure is about **120/80 mm Hg** (120 mm Hg is the systolic pressure; 80 mm Hg is the diastolic pressure). However, it can be affected by age and lifestyle.

Regular **aerobic exercise** strengthens the heart and helps maintain a normal blood pressure. A **healthy diet** can also help.

Excess weight (which can lead to obesity) due to lack of exercise and a poor diet puts a strain on the heart, which can lead to high blood pressure. Other factors that can damage the heart and blood vessels and lead to high blood pressure are…

- high stress levels
- smoking
- excess alcohol
- a diet which is high in saturated fat, sugar or salt.

HT Long-term high blood pressure is dangerous because the blood vessels can weaken and eventually burst. Burst blood vessels in the brain (called a stroke) or in the kidneys can cause permanent damage.

Low blood pressure, usually caused by weak pumping of the heart, can also be a serious problem. The blood does not circulate efficiently, so some parts of the body are deprived of glucose and oxygen. This can lead to dizziness and fainting, and cold hands and feet.

Pulse

Each time the heart beats, the arteries **pulse** (throb). This can be felt at certain points on the body where the arteries are close to the surface, e.g. the wrist or neck. The pulse rate is measured in beats per minute (**bpm**). A normal resting pulse rate for an adult is between 60bpm and 100bpm.

Fitness is normally assessed by measuring how quickly an individual's pulse rate **recovers** after exercise, i.e. by timing how long it takes for the pulse rate to return to the normal resting pulse rate for that individual. The fitter they are, the faster the recovery time.

Providing Oxygen to Cells

Living cells need energy to function, and during exercise they need much more energy.

The circulatory system carries **oxygen** and **glucose** to all the body's cells so that **energy** can be released through **aerobic respiration**.

Aerobic respiration takes place inside the cells. The oxygen and glucose molecules react and the glucose molecules are broken down to release energy trapped inside. It involves a combination of chemical reactions which can be simplified as a single equation:

$$\text{Glucose} + \text{Oxygen} \rightarrow \text{Carbon dioxide} + \text{Water} + \text{Energy}$$

HT $$C_6H_{12}O_6 + 6O_2 \rightarrow 6CO_2 + 6H_2O + \text{Energy}$$

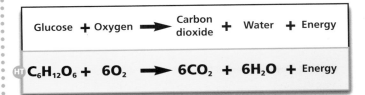

Muscle cells

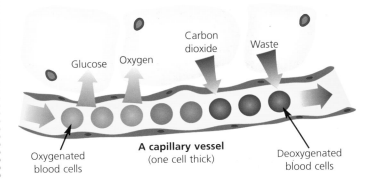

Glucose Oxygen Carbon dioxide Waste

Oxygenated blood cells

A capillary vessel (one cell thick)

Deoxygenated blood cells

Fit for Life

Effect of Exercise

As a person exercises, their breathing and pulse rate increase to deliver oxygen and glucose to the cells in the muscles more quickly (see graph below). Likewise, it helps to **remove** carbon dioxide produced during respiration more quickly.

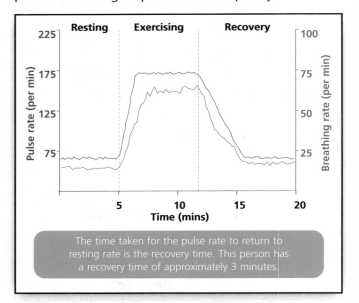

The time taken for the pulse rate to return to resting rate is the recovery time. This person has a recovery time of approximately 3 minutes.

However, there are limits to how much oxygen and glucose can be delivered, so there is another method of respiration, which can take place in addition to aerobic respiration. This is called **anaerobic respiration**.

Anaerobic Respiration

Anaerobic respiration takes place in the **absence of oxygen**. It quickly releases a small amount of energy through the **incomplete** breakdown of glucose.

Glucose ⟶ Lactic acid + A bit of energy

Anaerobic respiration occurs when the muscles are working so hard that the lungs and circulatory system cannot deliver enough **oxygen** to break down all the available glucose through aerobic respiration.

At this point, anaerobic respiration starts to take place **in addition** to aerobic respiration.

The **lactic acid** produced during anaerobic respiration is relatively toxic to the cells and can cause pain (cramp) and a sensation of fatigue in the muscles.

Because anaerobic respiration involves the incomplete breakdown of glucose, much less energy (about $\frac{1}{20}$) is released than in aerobic respiration. However, it can produce energy much faster over a short period of time, until fatigue sets in. This makes anaerobic respiration a real necessity in events which require a short, intense burst of energy, e.g. the 100 metre sprint.

Recovering After Anaerobic Respiration

Lactic acid produced during anaerobic respiration must be broken down fairly quickly to avoid cell damage and relieve the feeling of fatigue.

Immediately after anaerobic exercise…
- **the heart rate stays high** – pumping blood through the muscles to remove the lactic acid and transport it to the liver to be broken down
- **deep breathing continues** – ensuring enough oxygen is taken in to oxidise the lactic acid (producing carbon dioxide and water).

In effect, the body is taking in the oxygen that was not available for anaerobic respiration during exertion. This is why the process is sometimes referred to as repaying the **oxygen debt**.

A Balanced Diet

Food is essential for all living organisms because it supplies them with the **energy** and nutrients they need in order to grow and function.

Recommended Portions per Day

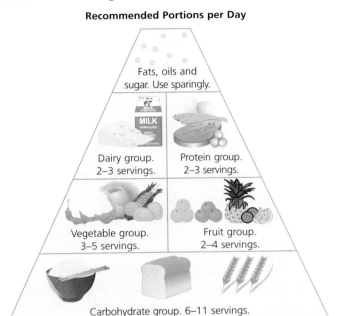

A **balanced diet** must contain…

- **carbohydrates** and **fats** to provide **energy**
- **protein** for **growth and repair of tissues** (and energy, if food is in short supply).

Other substances are also needed in a balanced diet to keep us healthy, although they do not provide energy. They include…

- **minerals**, such as **iron**, which is needed to make haemoglobin in red blood cells
- **vitamins**, such as **vitamin C**, which is needed to prevent scurvy
- **fibre**, which prevents **constipation**
- **water**, which prevents **dehydration**.

Everyone needs a balanced diet but people's diets vary greatly. This could be as a result of…

- beliefs about animal welfare, or their concerns about the effect of farming practices on food, e.g. vegetarians, vegans
- religious beliefs, e.g. the Muslim and Jewish faiths prohibit the eating of pig meat
- food allergies, e.g. people can be allergic to peanuts and may suffer anaphylactic shock as a result.

How Much Energy is Needed?

The amount of energy needed by an individual depends on their age, sex and activity levels.

To maintain a healthy body mass, it is important to **balance** the amount of **energy consumed** in food with the amount of **energy expended** (used up) through daily activity.

Many people in the developed world do not get this balance right and become very overweight or **obese**. Obesity is a major health problem. It can lead to arthritis (swollen and painful joints), heart disease, diabetes and breast cancer.

Body Mass Index

One way to show whether someone is underweight or overweight for their height is to calculate their **body mass index** (BMI).

$$\text{BMI} = \frac{\text{Mass (kg)}}{\text{Height}^2 \text{ (m}^2)}$$

Recommended BMI Chart

BMI	What it means
<18.5	Underweight – too light for your height
18.5–25	Ideal – correct weight range for your height
25–30	Overweight – too heavy for your height
30–40	Obese – much too heavy, health risks!

Example

Calculate a man's BMI if he is 1.65m tall and weighs 68kg.

$$\text{BMI} = \frac{\text{Mass (kg)}}{\text{Height}^2 \text{ (m}^2)}$$
$$= \frac{68}{1.65^2} = \frac{68}{2.7} = \mathbf{25}$$

The recommended BMI for his height (1.65m) is 18.5–25, so he is a healthy weight.

What's for Lunch?

Protein

Protein molecules are long chains of amino acids. There are different types of amino acids:

- **essential amino acids** – must be taken in by eating food (your body cannot make them)
- **non-essential amino acids** – can be made in the body.

Your diet should include the complete range of amino acids so that your body can make all the necessary proteins. Meat and fish are **first class proteins** because they contain all the different types of amino acids.

Very few vegetables contain all the necessary amino acids. Therefore, a vegetarian or vegan diet must include a wide variety of plant protein (especially beans and pulses) to make sure that all the amino acids are included.

A diet which does not contain enough protein will not allow normal growth. This is why it is important for teenagers to have a high protein diet.

In some parts of the world, food is in very short supply and people are starving. Often the only source of food they have is some sort of cereal like rice. Rice is not a good source of protein. In children, protein deficiency results in a disease called **kwashiorkor**. The muscles waste because the proteins in them are used for energy and the belly swells due to too much fluid.

How Much Protein?

The recommended daily allowance (**RDA**) of protein intake can be calculated using the formula:

RDA protein (g) **=** 0.75 **X** Body mass (kg)

Example

Calculate how much protein a woman who weighs 60kg would need. Use the formula…
RDA = 0.75 x Body mass
= 0.75 x 60 = **40g protein per day**

Eating Disorders

Problems with food can begin when people use it to help cope with painful situations or feelings. Feelings of low self-esteem, poor self-image or an unachievable desire for perfection can all lead to a poor diet. People might start using food as a source of comfort, restricting what they eat to try to lose weight or because it makes them feel more in control of their lives. When food is used in this way, it is called an **eating disorder**.

Eating disorders, and even some diets, are very **damaging** to the body, because the body is no longer getting the right balance of energy and nutrients it needs to function properly.

People who have **anorexia nervosa** restrict what they eat, and sometimes starve themselves. This can lead to extreme weight loss and poor growth, constipation and abdominal pains, dizzy spells and feeling faint, a bloated stomach, poor circulation, discoloured skin, irregular or no periods (in girls), and loss of bone mass, which can eventually develop into osteoporosis (brittle bones).

People who suffer from **bulimia nervosa** make themselves vomit, or take laxatives after eating, to get the food out of their system before it can be digested. This can lead to large weight fluctuations, a sore throat, tooth decay and bad breath, swollen salivary glands, poor skin condition and hair loss, irregular periods (in girls), tiredness, and an increased risk of problems with the heart and other internal organs.

What's for Lunch?

The Human Digestive System

Physical digestion includes chewing, and squeezing food in the stomach to break it into smaller pieces so that it can pass through the gut easily. The increase in surface area also helps chemical digestion take place quicker.

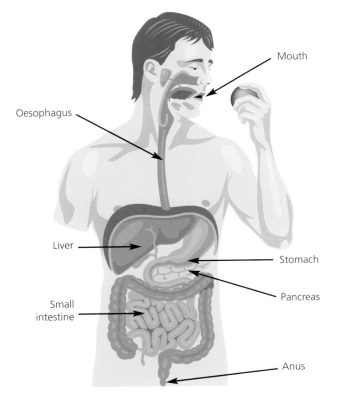

Mouth

Oesophagus

Liver

Stomach

Pancreas

Small intestine

Anus

Chemical digestion uses enzymes to break down large insoluble molecules, such as carbohydrates, fats and proteins, into smaller soluble molecules. These can then diffuse through the walls of the small intestine and into the blood plasma or lymph.

The large, insoluble molecules are digested by specific enzymes found in the **mouth**, **stomach** and **small intestine**.

In the mouth – carbohydrase enzymes break down large, insoluble **carbohydrates** (e.g. starch) into small soluble **sugars** (e.g. glucose).

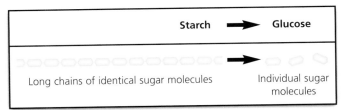

Starch → Glucose

Long chains of identical sugar molecules   Individual sugar molecules

In the stomach – protease enzymes break down large, insoluble **proteins** into small, soluble **amino acids**.

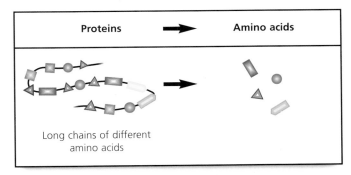

Proteins → Amino acids

Long chains of different amino acids

Hydrochloric acid is released by cells in the wall of the stomach. It **kills bacteria** in the food and creates **conditions** that help the enzymes to work effectively.

The **pancreas** produces **carbohydrases** and **proteases** to complete the digestion of **carbohydrates** and **proteins**. It also produces **lipase** enzymes to break down **fats** into **fatty acids** and **glycerol**.

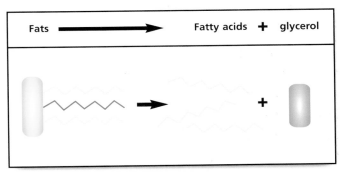

Fats → Fatty acids + glycerol

+

The small, soluble molecules produced by digestion are **absorbed** into the blood through the wall of the **small intestine** by **diffusion**.

HT **Fat** is hard to digest because it does not mix easily with water in the intestine. So, the body produces **bile** to **emulsify** the fat droplets, i.e. break down large droplets into smaller droplets to increase their surface area. This enables **lipase** enzymes to work much faster.

The bile is produced in the **liver** and then stored in the **gall bladder** before being released into the **small intestine**.

Keeping Healthy

Disease

Diseases are caused by **microorganisms** which attack and invade the body. **Infectious diseases** are spread from one person to another through unhygienic conditions or contact with an infected person. **Non-infectious diseases** cannot be caught from another person. They can be caused by…

- **poor diet**, e.g. a lack of vitamin C causes scurvy, and a lack of iron causes anaemia
- **organ malfunction**, e.g. the pancreas can stop producing insulin (which causes diabetes), or cells can mutate and become cancerous
- **genetic inheritance**, e.g. people can inherit the genes for a particular disease from their parent, e.g. red–green colour blindness.

Cancer

Cancer is a non-infectious disease caused by **mutations** in living cells. Making healthy lifestyle choices is one way to reduce the likelihood of cancer, for example…

- do not smoke – smoking causes lung cancer
- do not drink excess alcohol – alcohol is linked to cancer of the liver, gut and mouth
- avoid getting sunburnt – skin cells damaged by the Sun can become cancerous
- eat a healthy diet – a high-fibre diet can reduce the risk of bowel cancer.

HT Cancerous cells divide in an abnormal and uncontrolled way, forming lumps of cells called **tumours**. If a tumour grows in one place it is described as **benign**. However, if cells break off and secondary tumours start to grow in other parts of the body, they are described as **malignant**.

A person's **chance of survival** depends on the type of cancer they have. People with **breast** or **prostate** cancer have **high survival rates**, whereas people with **lung** or **stomach** cancer have very **low survival rates**. The chance of survival is greater if the cancer is diagnosed early and the patient is young.

Pathogens

Pathogens are disease-causing microorganisms. The different types are…

- **fungi**, e.g. athlete's foot
- **viruses**, e.g. flu
- **bacteria**, e.g. cholera
- **protozoa**, e.g. dysentery.

Malaria

Malaria is a disease caused by a **protozoan**, which is a **parasite**. Parasites live off other organisms, called **hosts**. In the case of malaria, humans are the hosts.

Malaria parasites can be sucked up from a human's bloodstream by mosquitoes (a **vector**). Once inside the mosquito, they mate and move from the gut to the salivary glands. When the mosquito bites another person, the malaria parasites are passed on into their bloodstream. They then head straight for the liver, where they mature and reproduce. The new generation of malaria then migrates to the blood and replicates in red blood cells, bursting them open. This damage leads to characteristic malaria fever and can sometimes result in death.

The parasite which causes malaria reproduces and matures much more quickly in warmer climates, and the mosquito vectors can only breed in stagnant water. This is why the pattern of malaria disease is linked to areas with warm, wet conditions.

HT The best way to prevent a disease like malaria spreading is to control the vectors. In countries where malaria is common, people sleep under mosquito nets and use insect repellents to avoid getting bitten by mosquitoes. Mosquitoes can be killed by spraying them with insecticide.

Defences Against Pathogens

The body has a number of defences to stop pathogens getting in:

- the **skin** acts as a barrier against microorganisms
- the **respiratory system** is lined with specialised cells that produce a **sticky, liquid mucus** that forms a **mucous membrane** which traps microorganisms. Tiny hairs called **cilia** move the mucus up to the mouth where it is swallowed
- the **stomach** produces hydrochloric acid which kills microorganisms on the food we eat
- the **blood** clots in wounds to prevent microorganisms from entering the bloodstream.

Dealing with Pathogens Inside the Body

If pathogens manage to enter the body, the white blood cells start fighting the invasion. (The symptoms of a disease are caused by pathogens **damaging cells** and **producing toxins (poisons)** before the white blood cells can destroy them.)

Phagocytes (see diagram ❶) are a type of white blood cell that move around in the bloodstream searching for pathogens. When they find some, they **engulf** and **digest** them. When we get an infected cut and pus develops, the yellow liquid is mainly white blood cells which are full of digested microbes.

Lymphocytes (see diagram ❷) are another type of white blood cell that make special substances called **antibodies** to attack pathogens. They recognise markers called **antigens** on the surface of the pathogen and produce antibodies which lock onto the antigens and kill the pathogens.

Specificity of Antibodies

Every pathogen has its own unique antigens. White blood cells make antibodies specifically for a particular antigen. So antibodies made to fight tetanus have no effect on whooping cough or cholera.

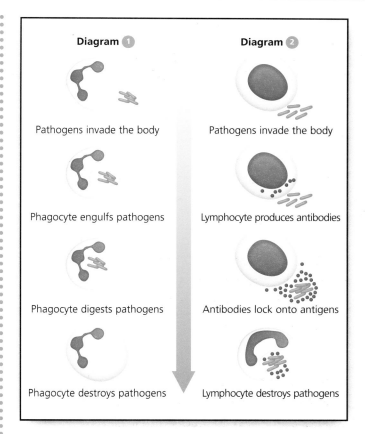

Diagram ❶
Pathogens invade the body
Phagocyte engulfs pathogens
Phagocyte digests pathogens
Phagocyte destroys pathogens

Diagram ❷
Pathogens invade the body
Lymphocyte produces antibodies
Antibodies lock onto antigens
Lymphocyte destroys pathogens

Natural (Passive) Immunity

Once white blood cells are sensitised to a particular pathogen, they can produce the necessary antibodies much quicker if the same pathogen is detected again. This provides future protection against the disease and is called **natural** or **passive immunity**.

Active Immunity

Immunisation provides immunity to a disease, without the person being infected by it as follows:

- a weakened or dead strain of the pathogen, which is incapable of multiplying inside a person, is injected
- the presence of the antigens on the modified pathogen triggers the production of specific antibodies by the white blood cells (even though they are harmless)
- long after the pathogen has been dealt with, the white blood cells which produced the antibodies capable of attacking them remain 'sensitised'. This means they can produce more antibodies very quickly if the same pathogen is detected again.

Keeping Healthy

Immunisation

Benefits
• It protects against diseases which could kill or cause disability, e.g. polio, measles.   • If everybody is vaccinated the disease cannot spread and eventually dies out. (This is what happened to smallpox.)

Risk
• An individual could have a bad reaction to the vaccine.

Some research has linked the MMR (mumps, measles and rubella) vaccine to children developing bowel problems and autism. As a result, lots of parents decided not to vaccinate their children. However, the number of cases of measles then immediately began to rise.

Treating Diseases with Drugs

Diseases caused by bacteria or fungi (not viruses) can be treated using antibiotics. These are drugs that kill the pathogen.

Antibiotics are very effective at killing bacteria. However, there are some bacteria which are **naturally resistant** to particular antibiotics.

It is important for patients to follow instructions carefully and take the full course of antibiotics to give them the best possible chance of killing all the bacteria.

If doctors over-prescribe antibiotics, all the bacteria in a population are killed off except for the resistant ones, which will then spread. The antibiotic then becomes useless. MRSA is a bacteria which has become resistant to most antibiotics making it a dangerous microorganism that the media has dubbed a **superbug**.

Drug Testing

New drugs have to be developed all the time to combat different diseases. The drugs must be tested to make sure that they are **effective** and **safe**. A drug can be tested using…

- **computer models** to predict how it will affect cells, based on known information about how the body works and the effects of similar drugs
- **animals** to see how it affects living organisms (many people object to this on the grounds of animal cruelty)
- **human tissue** (grown in a laboratory) to see how it affects human cells (some people object to human tissue being grown in this way because they believe it is unnatural and wrong).

Finally, the drug must be tested on healthy volunteers, and on volunteers who have the relevant disease. Some of them are given the new drug and some are given a **placebo** (an inactive pill). The effects of the drug can then be compared to the effects of taking the placebo.

In a **blind trial** the volunteers do not know whether they have been given the new drug or the placebo. This eliminates any psychological factors and helps to provide a **fair comparison**.

In a **double blind trial** neither the volunteers nor the doctors know which pill has been given. This eliminates **all** bias from the test, because the doctors cannot influence the volunteers' response in any way.

Although scientists conduct lots of tests beforehand to determine how the drugs will affect humans, drug trials like these can never be completely safe.

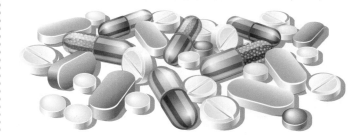

Nerve Cells (Neurones)

Neurones are **specially adapted cells** that can carry a **nerve impulse**. This is carried in the axon. There are three types of neurone:

1 A **sensory neurone** carries nerve impulses from the receptors to the brain.

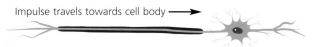

Impulse travels towards cell body →

2 A **motor neurone** carries nerve impulses from the brain to the muscles and glands.

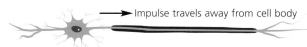

→ Impulse travels away from cell body

3 A **relay neurone** makes connections between neurones inside the brain and spinal cord.

Impulse travels first towards and then away from cell body

HT Motor neurones are specially adapted to carry out their function. They have…

- an **elongated** (long) shape to make connections from one part of the body to another
- an insulating **sheaf** which speeds up the nerve impulse
- **branched endings** (dendrites) which allow a single neurone to act on many muscle fibres.

There is a small gap between neurones called a **synapse**. An electrical impulse travels down a neurone until it reaches a synapse. A transmitter substance is then released across the synapse. The transmitter binds with receptor molecules on the next neurone, causing an electrical impulse to be released in that neurone.

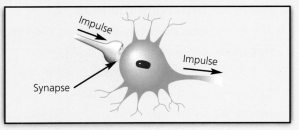

Impulse

Impulse

Synapse

The Nervous System

The nervous system allows organisms to **react** to their surroundings and **coordinate** their behaviour. The nervous system can be divided into the **central nervous system** and the **peripheral nervous system**.

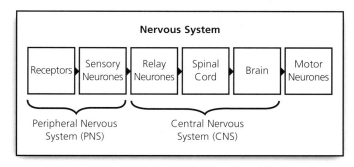

Nervous System

| Receptors | Sensory Neurones | Relay Neurones | Spinal Cord | Brain | Motor Neurones |

Peripheral Nervous System (PNS)

Central Nervous System (CNS)

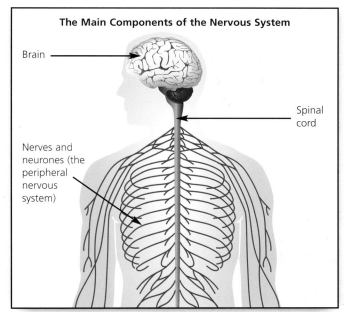

The Main Components of the Nervous System

Brain

Spinal cord

Nerves and neurones (the peripheral nervous system)

Receptors

Receptors are the specialised nerve endings that respond to stimuli. The different types are…

- light receptors in the eyes
- sound receptors in the ears
- change of position receptors in the ears (for balance)
- taste receptors on the tongue
- smell receptors in the nose
- touch, pressure, pain and temperature receptors in the skin.

Effectors are the **muscles** or **glands** that make the change in response to the signal from the receptor.

Keeping in Touch

Voluntary Action

Voluntary responses are under the **conscious control** of the **brain**, i.e. the person **decides** how to react to a stimulus. For example, if an insect landed on your thigh (stimulus), you would think about it and flick it away. The pathway for processing the information and then acting upon it is…

stimulus → receptor → sensory neurone → coordinator → motor neurone → effector → response.

Reflex Action

Reflex actions (or involuntary responses) bypass the brain to give **fast, automatic responses** to a stimulus, which help to protect the body from harm. The pathway for receiving and acting on information is…

stimulus → receptor → sensory neurone → coordinator → relay neurone → motor neurone → effector → response.

Some useful reflex actions include…
- pupil reflex automatically controls the amount of light that enters the eye (prevents damage to retina)
- knee jerk reaction
- withdrawing your hand from a hot plate to prevent you from getting burnt.

Vision

Some animals have eyes positioned close together on the front of their head, like humans. This is called **binocular vision**, and is usually found in predators, e.g. tigers. Each eye has a limited field of view but where the fields of view overlap, the brain interprets the information and creates a 3D image. This means the animal can judge distance and speed quite accurately.

Some animals have eyes set on either side of their head. This is called **monocular vision**, and is usually found in prey. Each eye has a wide field of view, so as well as being able to see to each side, the animal can also see behind and in front. However, there is very little overlap in the fields of view so it is difficult for the animal to judge distance or speed.

Voluntary Action
1. **Pressure receptors** in the skin of your thigh detect an insect crawling on you.
2. These cause an **impulse** to travel along a **sensory neurone** to the…
3. … **spinal cord**. Here, another sensory neurone carries the impulse to the **brain** (coordinator).
4. The brain thinks about this and decides to flick the insect away with the left hand.
5. An impulse is sent down a **motor neurone** in the spinal cord…
6. … and causes an impulse to be sent out of the spinal cord via another motor neurone…
7. … to a muscle (an **effector**) in the hand. This causes the hand to move and flick away the insect (a **response**).

Reflex Action

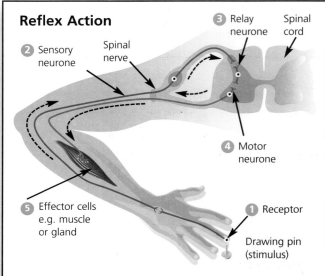

1. A **receptor** is stimulated by the pin (stimulus)…
2. … causing impulses to pass along a **sensory neurone** into the **spinal cord** (the coordinator in reflex actions).
3. The sensory neurone synapses with a **relay neurone**, **bypassing the brain**.
4. The relay neurone synapses with a **motor neurone**, sending impulses down it…
5. … to the muscles (**effectors**) causing them to contract and remove the hand in **response** to the pin.

The Eye

The eye is a complicated sense organ, which focuses light onto light-sensitive receptor cells in the retina. These are then stimulated and cause nerve impulses to pass along sensory neurones to the brain.

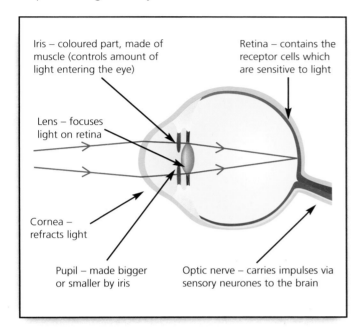

Iris – coloured part, made of muscle (controls amount of light entering the eye)

Retina – contains the receptor cells which are sensitive to light

Lens – focuses light on retina

Cornea – refracts light

Pupil – made bigger or smaller by iris

Optic nerve – carries impulses via sensory neurones to the brain

Focusing

The **cornea** and **lens refract** rays of light, so they converge (come together) at a single point and produce a **clear image** on the **retina**.

Eye Defects

The most common eye defects are…
- **long sight**
- **short sight**
- **red–green colour blindness** (inherited condition).

We see in colour because specialised cells in the retina detect red, green and blue light. In people with red-green colour blindness, some of these cells are missing.

Long and short sight are caused by the eyeball or the lens being the wrong shape, so the light rays cannot be accurately focused on the retina. Eyesight tends to get worse with age. This is because as the eye muscles get older they lose the ability to change the shape of the eye and focus.

The **lens** is a clear, flexible bag of fluid surrounded by circular ciliary muscles that change the shape of the lens (accommodation). **Suspensory ligaments** attach the lens to the ciliary muscles.

Light rays reflected by a **near** object **diverge** (are reflected out in all directions), so…
- the ciliary muscles **contract**
- the suspensory ligaments go **slack**
- the lens becomes **short and fat**
- light is **refracted a lot** to focus on the retina.

Light rays reflected by a **distant** object are almost **parallel** when they reach the eye, so…
- the ciliary muscles **relax**
- the suspensory ligaments become **taut**
- the lens becomes **long and thin**
- light is only **refracted a little** to focus on the retina.

Focus on a distant object

Focus on a near object

Long sight is caused by an eyeball that is too short or a lens that stays long and thin (it does not change shape properly). It can be corrected by a **convex** lens which **converges** the light rays from close objects so that they focus on the retina.

Short sight is caused by an eyeball that is too long, or weak ciliary muscles which cannot pull the lens into a thin, flat shape. It can be corrected by a **concave** lens which **diverges** the light rays so that they focus on the retina.

Corrective lenses can be worn as contact lenses or glasses. Some people opt for laser surgery to change the shape of the cornea and lens.

Slow or poor eyesight in older people is the result of poor eye accommodation.

Drugs and You

Drugs

Drugs are chemicals that affect the way the body works. They can affect the mind or the body (or both) and are used for **medicine** and **pleasure**. Some drugs used for pleasure are legally acceptable, e.g. tobacco and alcohol, whereas others are illegal, e.g. ecstasy and cocaine.

Illegal drugs are **harmful**. They can have very bad side effects and can lead to **addiction** and even **death**.

Even medicines can have bad side effects or be deadly if used incorrectly. This is why some can only be obtained on prescription.

- **Stimulants**, e.g. caffeine, nicotine, ecstasy
  - increased brain activity helps to combat depression
  - increased alertness and perception
  - caffeine and nicotine can be addictive.
- **Depressants or sedatives**, e.g. alcohol, solvents, tranquillisers (like temazepam)
  - decreased brain activity makes you feel tired and slows down your reactions
  - lethargy and forgetfulness.
- **Pain killers or anaesthetics**, e.g. aspirin, heroin, ketamine
  - reduces pain felt (nerve impulses blocked)
  - can be very addictive.
- **Performance-enhancing drugs**, e.g. anabolic steroids
  - increased muscle development (sometimes abused in sport).
- **Hallucinogens**, e.g. cannabis, LSD
  - distorted perceptions, sensations and emotions.

Drug Classification

In the UK, illegal drugs are **classified** into three main categories under the **Misuse of Drugs Act**.

- **Class A** drugs, e.g. heroin, cocaine, ecstasy, and LSD, are the most dangerous and carry heavy prison sentences and fines for possession.
- **Class B** drugs include amphetamines, e.g. speed and barbiturates.
- **Class C** drugs, e.g. tranquilisers, anabolic steroids and cannabis, are less dangerous and have lower penalties.

HT This three tier system of classification can be misleading. Some people think that it is all right to use drugs like cannabis because they are 'only' in Class C. It is important to remember that they are still illegal and still have associated health risks.

Stimulants and Depressants

Stimulants increase the amount of **transmitter substance** released at synapses in the nervous system. This increases the level of nervous activity taking place in the brain, giving rise to feelings of energy, alertness and euphoria.

Depressants block or reduce the amount of transmitter substance in the synapse. This reduces brain activity, slowing down reactions and making a person feel dopey, subdued or drowsy.

Addiction and Rehabilitation

An **addiction** is a **psychological need** for something, which means you always want more. As an addict's body becomes more used to the drug, it develops a **tolerance** to it. In other words, the addict needs higher doses of the drug to get the same effects. If a drug addict stops taking the drug they can suffer **withdrawal symptoms**, which include both **psychological problems**, e.g. **cravings**, and **physical problems**, e.g. sweating, shaking, nausea.

Rehabilitation is the process by which an addict gradually learns to live without the drug. This takes a long time because both their body and mind have to adapt.

Alcohol and tobacco are both legal drugs but they still have serious effects on health.

Drugs and You

Alcohol

Alcohol contains the chemical ethanol, which is a **depressant** and causes **slow reactions**. The **short-term effects** on the brain and nervous system can lead to lack of balance and muscle control, blurred vision, slurred speech, poor judgement and vasodilation (the blood vessels widen, increasing blood flow and heat loss). **Excess** alcohol can lead to **unconsciousness** and even **coma** or **death**.

The **long-term effects** of alcohol can be **cirrhosis** (liver damage, due to the liver having to work hard to remove the toxic alcohol from the body) or **brain damage** (due to dehydration).

A **unit** of alcohol is **10cm³** of pure alcohol. The advised weekly intake for men is 21 units and for women it is 14 units. The units in drinks are as follows:

- pint of ordinary strength lager, bitter or cider – 2 units
- pint of strong lager – 3 units
- large glass (175 cm³) of wine – 2 units
- pub measure of spirits – 1 unit
- alcopop (approx. 275 cm³) – 1.5 units.

The **legal limit** for drinking and driving is 80 milligrams of **alcohol** in 100 millilitres of blood (80mg/100ml). This cannot easily be converted into units because the effects of alcohol depend on many factors including age, sex, height and how much food has been eaten. This legal limit has been set because alcohol slows reaction times, increasing the chance of accidents. It is important to remember that even one alcoholic drink affects your ability to react, so it is better to not drink anything at all before driving.

Tobacco

Tobacco contains tar, carbon monoxide and **nicotine**, which is very **addictive**. These chemicals damage the **cilia** (ciliated epithelial cells), which line the airways (trachea), so they cannot remove the mucus, tar and dirt from the lungs. This leads to a **smoker's cough**. Excess coughing can damage the alveoli and cause **emphysema**.

Bronchitis is common in smokers because the mucus in their lungs leaves them susceptible to infection, and they are often breathless because their cells are not getting enough oxygen – the haemoglobin in their red blood cells picks up **carbon monoxide** instead of **oxygen**.

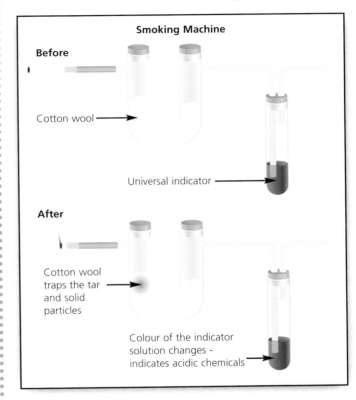

Smoking Machine

Before

Cotton wool

Universal indicator

After

Cotton wool traps the tar and solid particles

Colour of the indicator solution changes - indicates acidic chemicals

Carbon monoxide and nicotine are gases which cannot be detected in a simple smoking machine like this one, but are analysed by more sophisticated detectors. Carbon monoxide also encourages fat deposits in arteries leading to arteriosclerosis. The arteries around the heart become blocked which can lead to heart disease and, ultimately, a heart attack.

Tar contains chemicals that are irritants and carcinogens. Particulates from the cigarette (see experiment below) accumulate in living tissue which can cause mouth, throat, lung and oesophagus **cancer**. Other chemicals in cigarette smoke cause **high blood pressure** and increase the chance of **blocked blood vessels**, which cause **strokes** and **heart disease**.

Babies born to mothers who smoke throughout pregnancy often have lower, less healthy, **birth weights**.

Staying in Balance

Homeostasis

The body has automatic control systems to maintain a constant internal environment (**homeostasis**) to ensure that cells can function efficiently. It balances inputs and outputs and removes waste products to ensure that the correct levels of temperature, water, oxygen and carbon dioxide are maintained.

Temperature Control

Since **enzymes** work best at **37°C** (in humans), it is essential that the body remains very close to this temperature. Heat produced through respiration is used to maintain the body temperature.

If body temperature becomes too high, the blood flows closer to the skin so heat can be transferred to the environment. This is also done by sweating – evaporation of sweat requires heat energy from the skin. Getting too hot is very dangerous. If too much water is lost through sweating, the body becomes **dehydrated**. This can lead to **heat stroke** and even death.

If the body temperature falls too low, the blood flow near the skin is reduced, sweating stops and muscles start making tiny contractions, commonly known as shivers. These contractions need energy from respiration and heat is released as a by-product.

Getting too cold can also be fatal. **Hypothermia** is when the body temperature drops too far below 37°C. This causes unconsciousness and sometimes death. If you start to feel cold, you should put on some more clothing and do some exercise.

Body temperature readings can be taken from the mouth, ear, skin surface, finger or anus. Although an anal temperature reading is the most accurate, it is normally only used in hospitals. Digital recording probes and thermal imaging are also used in hospitals. At home, heat-sensitive strips that are placed on forehead are an alternative to thermometers.

HT Vasodilation and Vasoconstriction

Blood temperature is monitored by the brain, which switches various temperature control mechanisms on and off. **Vasodilation** and **vasoconstriction** are the widening and narrowing (respectively) of the blood vessels close to the skin's surface to increase or reduce heat loss.

Negative Feedback

Negative feedback occurs frequently in homeostasis. It involves the automatic reversal of a change in condition. For example, temperature falls too low, so the brain switches on mechanisms to increase it. The temperature then becomes too high, so the brain switches on mechanisms to lower it. Just like a central heating thermostat!

Core body temperature too high

Thermoregulatory Centre

Core body temperature too low

Heat loss by radiation

Sweat

Sweat gland

Body temperature needs to decrease – blood vessels in skin dilate (become wider) causing greater heat loss, as more heat is lost from the surface of the skin by radiation.

Shunt vessel closed – greater blood flow through superficial capillary.

Sweating stopped

Sweat gland

Body temperature needs to increase – blood vessels in skin constrict (become narrower) reducing heat loss, as less heat is lost from the surface of the skin by radiation.

Shunt vessel open – reduced blood flow through superficial capillary.

Hormones

Hormones are chemicals released by **endocrine** glands. They are released directly into the **bloodstream** and travel around the body to their **target organs**. This is much slower than a nervous impulse, which is relayed directly to the target organs.

In females, the hormone **oestrogen** is released by the ovaries. In males, the hormone **testosterone** is released by the testes. In both males and females, the hormone **insulin** is released by the pancreas.

Diabetes

Diabetes is caused by the **pancreas** not producing enough of the hormone insulin, which controls blood sugar levels. This can lead to blood sugar levels rising fatally **high** and result in a **coma**, so blood sugar has to be **controlled** by **injecting** insulin or controlling the amount of **sugar** in the diet.

Insulin helps to regulate blood sugar levels by converting excess **glucose** in the blood to **glycogen** in the liver.

Before injecting insulin, a person with diabetes tests the amount of sugar in their blood. If they have had food containing a lot of sugar then a bigger dose of insulin is required to reduce the blood sugar level. If they intend to exercise, then a smaller dose is required as they will use up a lot of sugar (for energy).

Secondary Sexual Characteristics

During **puberty** (ages 10–16 in girls, and 12–17 in boys) the sex organs begin to produce the **sex hormones** which cause the development of the **secondary sexual characteristics**.

In girls, the hormone oestrogen is released from the ovaries. This leads to the start of ovulation and menstruation (i.e. periods); growth of breasts; widening of hips; growth of pubic and armpit hair.

In boys, testosterone is released from the testes which leads to the production of sperm; development of muscles and penis; deepening of voice; growth of pubic, facial and body hair.

The Menstrual Cycle

Whilst a woman is fertile (between approximately 13 and 50 years of age), the lining of her uterus is replaced every month.

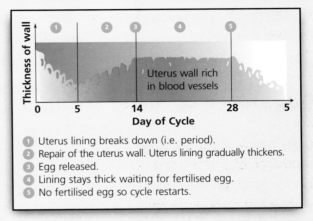

1. Uterus lining breaks down (i.e. period).
2. Repair of the uterus wall. Uterus lining gradually thickens.
3. Egg released.
4. Lining stays thick waiting for fertilised egg.
5. No fertilised egg so cycle restarts.

There are two hormones involved in these changes:

- **oestrogen** – stimulates repair of the uterus wall and thickening of uterus lining
- **progesterone** – maintains the uterus lining until end of cycle
- **oestrogen and progesterone** – work together to control ovulation.

Artificial Control of Fertility

Fertility in women can be artificially controlled using…
- hormones that stimulate the release of eggs from the ovaries – **fertility drugs**
- hormones that prevent the release of eggs from the ovaries – **contraceptive pills**.

The contraceptive pill contains hormones that are found in the body naturally during pregnancy. When these hormones are detected the ova stop releasing eggs.

Infertility due to the lack of eggs can be treated by the use of female sex hormones.

Gene Control

Genetic Information

The nuclei of living cells contain **chromosomes** which are made up of a string of genes. Different **genes** control the development of different characteristics by issuing instructions to the cell.

Chromosomes are long lengths of **DNA** (deoxyribonucleic acid). The DNA molecule itself consists of **two strands** which are coiled to form a **double helix**. The DNA molecules in a cell form a complete set of **instructions** on how the organism should be constructed and how its individual cells should work.

The instructions are in the form of a **chemical code** made up of the four **bases**, which hold the two strands of the molecule together. The order (or sequence) of the bases in a particular **region** of DNA (a gene) provides the **genetic code** that controls cell activity and the development of the related characteristic.

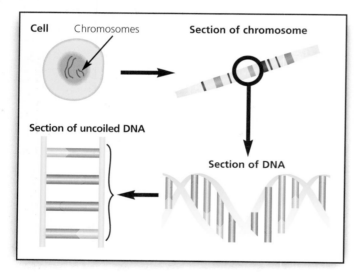

Reproduction

Most body cells have the **same number** of **chromosomes**, in matching **pairs** – humans have 23 pairs (46 chromosomes in total). However, the **gametes** (sex cells) contain individual chromosomes and therefore have exactly half the number of normal cells – 23 chromosomes in humans. So during **sexual reproduction**, when the male (sperm) and female (egg) gametes **fuse**, they produce a cell with the correct number of chromosomes.

This process increases the amount of **variation** in a species because genetic information from two parents is mixed together to produce a unique new individual.

The gametes from each parent all contain **different combinations of genes** and they fuse **randomly**. This is why siblings (brothers and sisters) can be quite different.

In **asexual reproduction**, all the genes come from one parent. The offspring, which are genetically identical to the parent and each other, are called **clones**.

Although each cell has a complete set of chromosomes, only some of the genes are **switched on** and used in any one cell. This is why cells are not all identical.

The order of the bases (**A**, **C**, **G** and **T**) in a gene represent the order in which **amino acids** should be assembled by the cells to make **proteins**. Many cell proteins are enzymes, which are catalysts that control the rates of reactions inside the cell. This is how the DNA controls the activities which go on inside the cell.

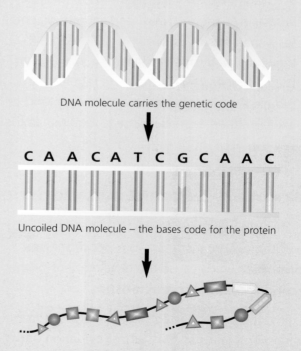

DNA molecule carries the genetic code

C A A C A T C G C A A C

Uncoiled DNA molecule – the bases code for the protein

Protein (chain of amino acids represented by the symbols)

Variation

Differences between individuals of the same species are described as **variation**. This may be due to **genetic** or **environmental** causes.

Genetic variations occur because individuals inherit different combinations of genes. Genetic variation between individuals can be caused by…

- mutations which alter the genes
- differences between individual gametes (eggs and sperm)
- random fusion of an egg with one out of millions of sperm at fertilisation.

Some examples of variation due to genetic causes are nose shape, eye colour, whether your earlobes are attached or detached, and hair colour.

Some variations are due to environmental causes, because individuals develop in different conditions, for example spoken language and scars.

Often variation is due to a **combination** of genetic and environmental causes, e.g. in characteristics like height, body mass and intelligence.

> **HT** Scientists are currently debating whether genetics or environment has the greatest influence in the development of characteristics like intelligence, health and sporting ability. It is unlikely that any characteristics are the sole result of one factor.

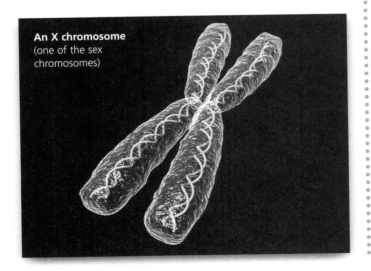

An X chromosome
(one of the sex chromosomes)

Inheritance of Sex

Gender (in mammals) is inherited via the **sex chromosomes**; one of the 23 pairs present in humans. The chromosomes are labelled **X** or **Y**. It is the presence of the Y chromosome which determines the gender of an individual: **XX = female**; **XY = male**.

> **HT** All egg cells carry X chromosomes. Half the sperm carry X chromosomes and half carry Y chromosomes. The sex of an individual depends on whether the egg is fertilised by an X-carrying sperm or a Y-carrying sperm.
> If an X sperm fertilises the egg it will become a girl. If a Y sperm fertilises the egg it will become a boy. The chances of these events are equal, which results in approximately equal numbers of male and female offspring.

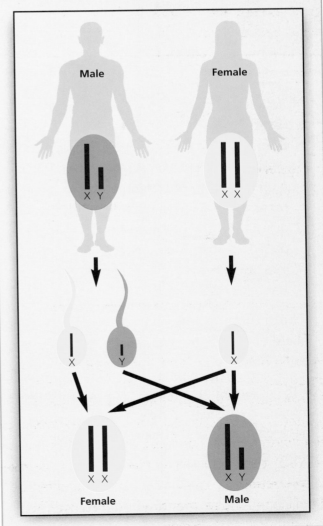

Who Am I?

The Terminology of Inheritance

Genes can have different **alleles** (versions). For example, the gene for eye colour has two alleles: brown and blue. Similarly, the gene for tongue rolling has two alleles: being able to roll your tongue and not being able to roll your tongue.

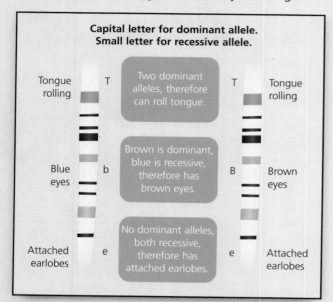

Capital letter for dominant allele.
Small letter for recessive allele.

Tongue rolling — T — Two dominant alleles, therefore can roll tongue.

Blue eyes — b — Brown is dominant, blue is recessive, therefore has brown eyes.

Attached earlobes — e — No dominant alleles, both recessive, therefore has attached earlobes.

T — Tongue rolling
B — Brown eyes
e — Attached earlobes

Alleles are described as being **dominant** or **recessive**:

- **dominant** – an allele which controls the development of a characteristic even if it is present on only one chromosome in a pair
- **recessive** – an allele which controls the development of a characteristic only if a dominant allele is not present, i.e. if the recessive allele is present on both chromosomes in a pair.

If **both chromosomes** in a pair contain the **same allele** of a gene, the individual is described as being **homozygous** for that gene or condition.

If the chromosomes in a pair contain **different alleles** of a gene, the individual is **heterozygous** for that gene or condition.

When a characteristic is determined by just one pair of alleles, as with eye colour and tongue rolling, it is called **monohybrid inheritance**.

Genetic Diagrams

Genetic diagrams are used to show all the possible combinations of alleles and outcomes for a particular gene. They use **capital letters for dominant alleles** and **lower case letters for recessive alleles**.

Example

For eye colour, brown is dominant and blue is recessive so B represents a brown allele and b represents a blue allele.

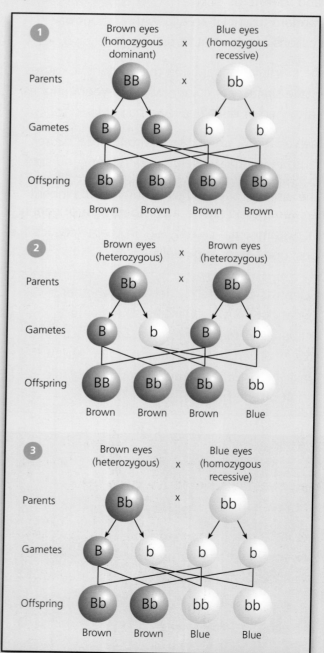

1
Brown eyes (homozygous dominant) x Blue eyes (homozygous recessive)
Parents: BB x bb
Gametes: B B b b
Offspring: Bb Bb Bb Bb
Brown Brown Brown Brown

2
Brown eyes (heterozygous) x Brown eyes (heterozygous)
Parents: Bb x Bb
Gametes: B b B b
Offspring: BB Bb Bb bb
Brown Brown Brown Blue

3
Brown eyes (heterozygous) x Blue eyes (homozygous recessive)
Parents: Bb x bb
Gametes: B b b b
Offspring: Bb Bb bb bb
Brown Brown Blue Blue

Inherited Diseases

Some diseases are caused by a 'faulty' gene, which means they can be **inherited** (i.e. they can be passed from one generation of a family to the next). Some examples include...

- **red–green colour blindness**, where the specialised cells in the eye cannot distinguish between red and green light
- **sickle cell anaemia**, which causes red blood cells to become sickle-shaped leading to circulatory problems and oxygen deficiency
- **cystic fibrosis**, which causes cell membranes to produce too much mucus resulting in blocked airways.

Cystic fibrosis is an example of a disease which is due to a recessive characteristic. Two parents could appear to be completely healthy and unaffected by the disease, but if they both have a recessive gene for the disease, one of their children could inherit the disease from them. (The parents do not have the disease themselves because their dominant 'normal' genes protect them.)

An affected child is likely to have a reduced quality of life and a reduced life expectancy. They will need life-long care and medication. However, modern drugs enable many affected people to lead happy and productive lives.

Mutations

New forms of genes can arise from **mutations** (changes) in existing genes. This occurs when one of the bases that codes for the gene changes to another base.

Mutations are usually **harmful** but can sometimes be beneficial. They occur naturally and spontaneously but their frequency is increased by exposure to...

- **ultraviolet light**
- **radioactive substances**
- **X-rays**
- **certain chemicals**.

More on Inherited Diseases

Conditions such as cystic fibrosis are mostly caused by **faulty alleles** that are **recessive**.

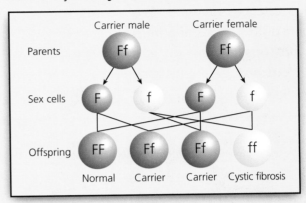

Knowing that there is a 1 in 4 chance that their child might have cystic fibrosis gives parents the opportunity to make decisions about whether to take the risk and have a child. However, this is a very difficult decision to make.

More about Mutations

Mutations are changes to the structure of the DNA molecule. The mutations change (or prevent) the sequence of amino acids that the genes usually code for, so different proteins are made, which cause the nature of that particular gene to change. The 'new' gene can then be passed on to 'daughter' cells through cell division.

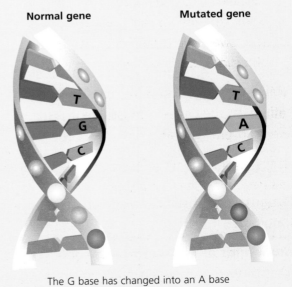

The G base has changed into an A base

Fundamental Chemical Concepts

For this unit, you need to have a good understanding of the following concepts (ideas).

Atoms

All substances are made up of **atoms**. Atoms contain three types of particles:

- **protons**
- **neutrons** (except hydrogen!)
- **electrons**.

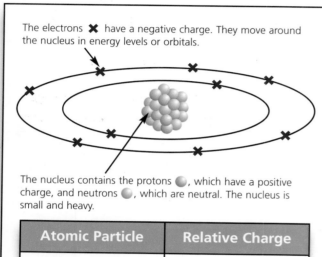

The electrons ✖ have a negative charge. They move around the nucleus in energy levels or orbitals.

The nucleus contains the protons ⬤, which have a positive charge, and neutrons ⬤, which are neutral. The nucleus is small and heavy.

Atomic Particle		Relative Charge
Proton	⬤	+1
Neutron	⬤	0
Electron	✖	-1

Atoms always contain equal numbers of electrons (negatively charged) and protons (positively charged) so they are electrically neutral (i.e. they have no overall charge).

Elements and Compounds

Elements are substances made up of just **one** type of atom.

Compounds are substances formed from the atoms of **two** or more elements, which have been **joined** together by a chemical bond.

There are two ways they can do this:

- **covalent bonds** – two atoms share a pair of electrons (The atoms in molecules are held together by covalent bonds.)
- **ionic bonds** – atoms turn into ions (become charged by losing or gaining electrons) and then the positive ions attract the negative ions.

Chemical Reactions

In a **chemical reaction** the substances that you start with are called **reactants**. During the reaction, the atoms in the reactants are rearranged in some way to form new substances called **products**. No atoms are lost or gained during the reaction.

Chemical Symbols

Each element is represented by a different **chemical symbol**, e.g.

- Fe for iron
- Na for sodium.

These symbols are all arranged in the **periodic table**.

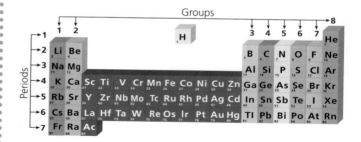

Formulae

Chemical symbols are used with numbers to write **formulae** that represent molecules of compounds, e.g.

- H_2O, water
- CO_2, carbon dioxide
- NH_3, ammonia.

Formulae are used to show…

- the different **elements** in a compound
- the **number of atoms** of each element in one molecule of the compound.

Fundamental Chemical Concepts

Sodium chloride

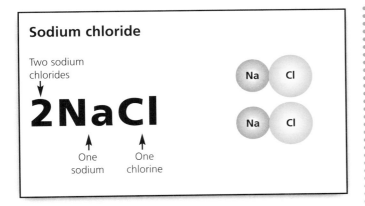

Two sodium chlorides

2NaCl

One sodium → Na
One chlorine → Cl

Sulfuric acid

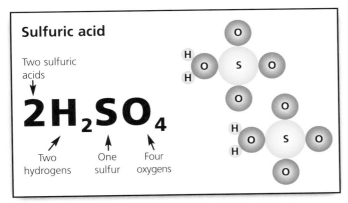

Two sulfuric acids

2H₂SO₄

Two hydrogens
One sulfur
Four oxygens

If there are **brackets** around part of the formula, everything inside the brackets is multiplied by the number outside, e.g.

Magnesium hydroxide

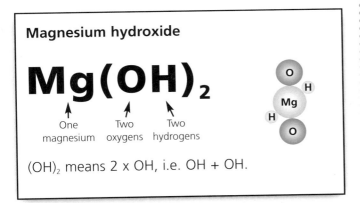

Mg(OH)₂

One magnesium
Two oxygens
Two hydrogens

$(OH)_2$ means 2 x OH, i.e. OH + OH.

Calcium nitrate

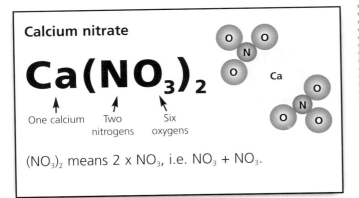

Ca(NO₃)₂

One calcium
Two nitrogens
Six oxygens

$(NO_3)_2$ means 2 x NO₃, i.e. NO₃ + NO₃.

HT You need to know the formulae for the following compounds:

- **carbon dioxide, CO_2**
- **carbon monoxide, CO**
- **ethane, C_2H_6**
- **methane, CH_4**
- **oxygen, O_2**
- **water, H_2O**

Try to learn as many of the formulae in this book as you can – it will help you in your exams.

Displayed Formulae

A displayed formula is another way to show the composition of a molecule, e.g. ethanol, C_2H_5OH.

$$
\begin{array}{ccc}
 & H & H \\
 & | & | \\
H - & C - C & - O - H \\
 & | & | \\
 & H & H \\
\end{array}
$$

The displayed formula for an ethanol molecule (above) shows…

- the **different types of atom** in the molecule: carbon, hydrogen and oxygen
- the **number of each different type of atom**: one oxygen, two carbon atoms and six hydrogen atoms = 9 atoms
- the **covalent bonds** between the atoms.

Equations

Chemists use **equations** to show what has happened during a **chemical reaction**, with the **reactants** on one side and the **products** on the other.

Remember, no atoms are lost or gained during a chemical reaction. This means that the equation must be balanced: there must always be the same number of atoms of each element on both sides of the equation.

Fundamental Chemical Concepts

Balancing Equations

Example 1

	Reactants			Products
① Write a word equation	Magnesium	+	Oxygen	Magnesium oxide
② Substitute in formulae	**Mg**	+	**O$_2$**	**MgO**

③ Balance the equation
- First, we need to add another **MgO** to the product side to balance the **O**s.
- We now need to add another **Mg** on the reactant side to balance the **Mg**s.
- There are two magnesium atoms and two oxygen atoms on each side – **it is balanced**.

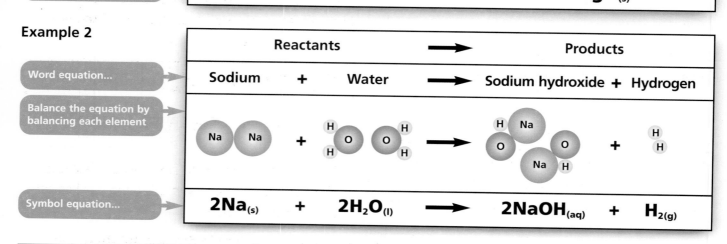

④ Write a balanced symbol equation

$$2Mg_{(s)} \quad + \quad O_2 \quad \longrightarrow \quad 2MgO_{(s)}$$

Example 2

	Reactants			Products
Word equation...	Sodium	+	Water	Sodium hydroxide + Hydrogen

Balance the equation by balancing each element

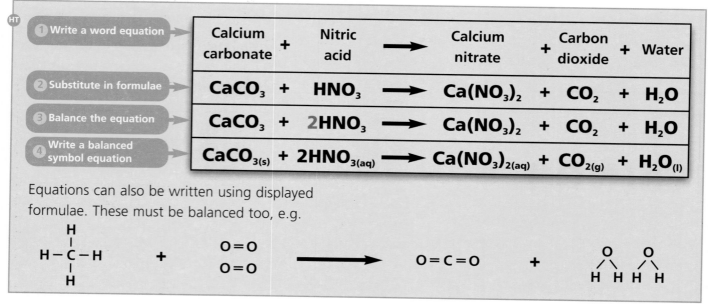

Symbol equation...

$$2Na_{(s)} \quad + \quad 2H_2O_{(l)} \quad \longrightarrow \quad 2NaOH_{(aq)} \quad + \quad H_{2(g)}$$

---

① Write a word equation

Calcium carbonate + Nitric acid ⟶ Calcium nitrate + Carbon dioxide + Water

② Substitute in formulae

$$CaCO_3 + HNO_3 \longrightarrow Ca(NO_3)_2 + CO_2 + H_2O$$

③ Balance the equation

$$CaCO_3 + 2HNO_3 \longrightarrow Ca(NO_3)_2 + CO_2 + H_2O$$

④ Write a balanced symbol equation

$$CaCO_{3(s)} + 2HNO_{3(aq)} \longrightarrow Ca(NO_3)_{2(aq)} + CO_{2(g)} + H_2O_{(l)}$$

Equations can also be written using displayed formulae. These must be balanced too, e.g.

H–C(–H)(–H)–H   +   O=O / O=O   ⟶   O=C=O   +   O(H H) O(H H)

Cooking Food

There are lots of different types of food. Some can be eaten **raw**, e.g. fruit and some vegetables, and others must be **cooked**, e.g. eggs and meat.

You can cook food by boiling, steaming, frying, grilling or heating in a conventional (normal) oven or microwave oven.

Food is cooked in order to…
- improve the flavour and taste
- improve the texture
- make it easier to digest
- kill microorganisms, to make it safer to eat.

Cooking food causes a **chemical change** to take place. When a chemical change occurs…
- **new substances** are formed from old ones
- there may be a **change in mass**
- there is often a substantial **energy change**, e.g. temperature rise or fall
- the change **cannot be reversed** easily.

Cooking Eggs and Meat

Eggs and **meat** contain lots of **protein**. The protein molecules **change shape** when they are heated. This causes the texture and appearance of the food to change, e.g. an egg changes colour and solidifies when it is heated.

(HT) The process that causes the protein molecules in eggs and meat to change shape during cooking is irreversible and is called **denaturing**.

heat

Protein molecule → Protein destroyed by heat

Cooking Potatoes

Potatoes are a good source of **carbohydrates**. When potatoes are cooked they soften and the flavour improves.

(HT) Because potatoes and other vegetables are plants, their cells have a rigid cell wall. During cooking, the heat breaks down this cell wall and starch is released, which the body can easily digest.

Baking Powder

Baking powder contains **sodium hydrogen carbonate**. When this is heated, it breaks down (**decomposes**) to make sodium carbonate and water, and **carbon dioxide** gas is given off. The word equation for the decomposition of sodium hydrogen carbonate is…

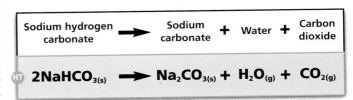

| Sodium hydrogen carbonate | → | Sodium carbonate | + | Water | + | Carbon dioxide |

(HT) $2NaHCO_{3(s)} \rightarrow Na_2CO_{3(s)} + H_2O_{(g)} + CO_{2(g)}$

Baking powder is added to cake mixture because the carbon dioxide gas given off when it is heated causes the cake to **rise**.

Limewater (**calcium hydroxide solution**) can be used to test for the presence of carbon dioxide. If carbon dioxide is present, the limewater will turn **milky**.

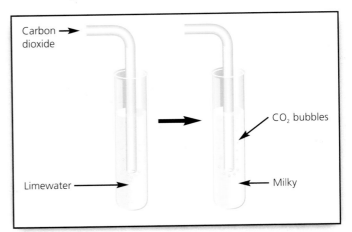

Carbon dioxide

CO_2 bubbles

Limewater

Milky

Food Additives

Additives

All the materials that make up food are **chemicals**. A material that is put in a food to improve it in some way is called a **food additive**.

Additives are given **E numbers** and can be seen on food labels. Ingredients are always listed in order of weight, with the greatest first.

INGREDIENTS:
Milk chocolate, Sugar, Modified starch, Colours (E104 Quinoline Yellow, E110 Sunset Yellow FCF, E120 Carminic acid, E122 Azorubine, E124 Cochineal Red A, E133 Brilliant Blue FCF, E171 Titanium dioxide), Glazing agents (E901 Beeswax, E903 Carnauba wax), Flavouring.

A small number of people find that they are **allergic** to certain food additives. This means that certain food additives are harmful to them.

The main types of food additives are listed below.
- **Antioxidants** – materials that stop the food reacting with oxygen in the air. They are usually added to foods containing fats or oils, e.g. sausages and bacon.
- **Food colours** – improve the appearance of the food.
- **Flavour enhancers** – help bring out the flavour of a food without adding a taste of their own.
- **Emulsifiers** – help to mix ingredients which would normally separate. Salad dressings and mayonnaise contain emulsifiers.

Emulsifiers

Oil and water do not mix. This is why emulsifiers have to be used. The molecules in an emulsifier have two ends: one end likes to be in water (**hydrophilic**) and the other end likes to be in oil (**hydrophobic**). The emulsifier joins the droplets together and keeps them mixed.

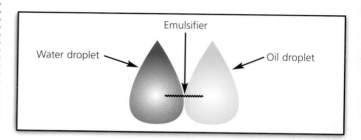

Water droplet / Emulsifier / Oil droplet

HT The diagram below shows the interaction between an emulsifier and water and oil. The **hydrophilic** end of the emulsifier molecule is **polar** and it bonds to the **polar water molecules**. The **hydrophobic** end of the emulsifier molecule is **non-polar** and it bonds to the **non-polar oil molecules**.

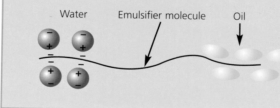

Water / Emulsifier molecule / Oil

Active Packaging

Active packaging can improve the **quality** of the product, e.g.
- some drinks cans have a base you can twist to trigger an endothermic reaction to cool the drink down by taking the heat out of the can
- some packages have a button you can press to trigger an exothermic reaction to heat the product up by giving out heat into the package.

It can also be used to improve the **safety** of the food, for example, adding a substance that absorbs water from inside a food package stops the growth of bacteria or moulds that would damage the food.

Perfumes

Smells are made of molecules which travel up your nose and stimulate sense cells.

A perfume must smell nice. In addition, it must…

- evaporate easily – so it can travel to your nose
- not be toxic – so it does not poison you
- not irritate – otherwise it would be uncomfortable on the skin
- not dissolve in water – otherwise it would wash off hands easily
- not react with water – otherwise it would react with perspiration.

There are many kinds of perfume. Some come from **natural** sources, such as plants and animals. Examples include lavender, rose, patchouli, pine and musk. Perfumes can also be **manufactured**. If they are manufactured they are known as **synthetic** perfumes.

Esters are a common family of compounds used as perfumes. An ester is made by reacting an alcohol with an organic acid. This produces an ester and water. A simple ester, ethyl ethanoate, is made by adding ethanoic acid to ethanol (see below).

Perfumes and cosmetics need to be tested to make sure they are not harmful. This testing is sometimes done on animals; some people are not happy about this. They argue that it is cruel to animals, and pointless because animals do not have the same body chemistry as humans and so results of the tests may not be useful. However, the tests could be useful to prevent humans from being harmed.

Perfumes are **volatile**: they evaporate easily.

The particles in a drop of perfume are held together by weak forces of attraction. The particles that escape have lots of energy and easily overcome the weak attraction.

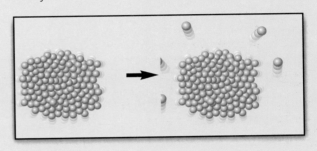

Ethanoic acid

Add 2 drops of concentrated sulfuric acid to speed up the reaction

Ethanol

Reaction mixture

The sodium carbonate solution removes any remaining acid

Sodium carbonate solution

Ester

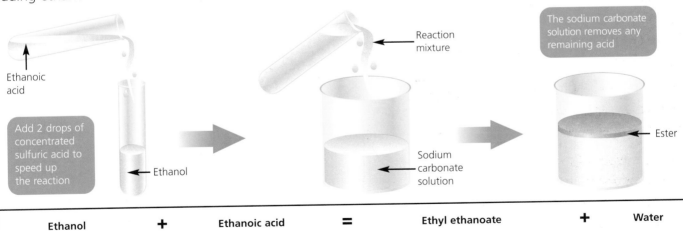

Ethanol	+	Ethanoic acid	=	Ethyl ethanoate	+	Water
C_2H_5OH	+	CH_3COOH	=	$C_2H_5OOCCH_3$	+	H_2O

Smells

Solvents

Nail varnish dissolves in ethyl ethanoate (nail varnish remover) but not in water.

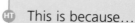 This is because…
- the attraction between water molecules is stronger than the attraction between water molecules and the particles in nail varnish
- the attraction between the particles in nail varnish is stronger than the attraction between water molecules and particles in nail varnish.

Below are some words that are used to describe substances:

- **Soluble substances** are substances that dissolve in a liquid, e.g. nail varnish is soluble in ethyl ethanoate.
- **Insoluble substances** are substances that do not dissolve in a liquid, e.g. nail varnish is insoluble in water.
- A **solvent** is the liquid into which a substance is dissolved, e.g. ethyl ethanoate is a solvent. (An ester can be used as a solvent.)
- The **solute** is the substance that gets dissolved, e.g. the nail varnish is a solute.
- A **solution** is what you get when you mix a solvent and a solute.

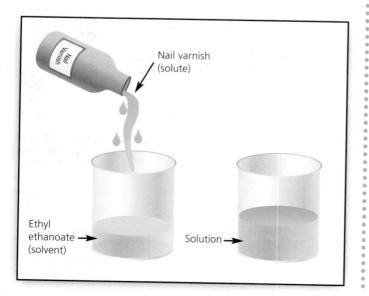

Nail varnish (solute)

Ethyl ethanoate (solvent)

Solution

Making a Solution

The diagram below shows what happens to the molecules when a solute dissolves.

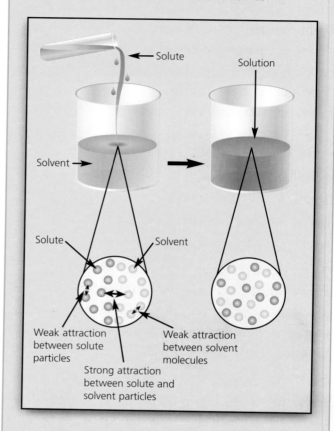

Solute

Solution

Solvent

Solute

Solvent

Weak attraction between solute particles

Weak attraction between solvent molecules

Strong attraction between solute and solvent particles

The solute particles separate from each other and **mix** with the solvent because the attraction between the solvent and the solute is so strong.

The following diagram shows what happens to the particles when a solute is insoluble.

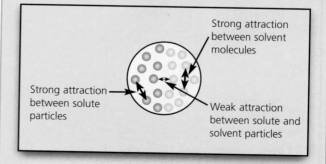

Strong attraction between solvent molecules

Strong attraction between solute particles

Weak attraction between solute and solvent particles

The solute particles do not separate as the attraction between the solvent and the solute is not strong enough.

Fossil Fuels

Crude oil, **coal** and **natural gas** are all **fossil fuels**. Fossil fuels are formed naturally, but it takes a very long time: millions of years!

All fossil fuels are **finite**, i.e. there are limited supplies. They are described as **non-renewable** because we are using them up much faster than new supplies can be formed. This means they will eventually run out.

Crude Oil

Crude oil is found trapped in **permeable** rock. To release the oil, a hole is drilled through the rock. If the oil is under pressure, it will flow out. If it is not under pressure, it has to be pumped out.

When crude oil is extracted it is a **thick, black, sticky liquid**. It is transported to a refinery through a pipeline or in oil tankers. This is a dangerous procedure: if the oil spills into the sea, it can have a devastating effect on wildlife.

Oil spills or **slicks** float on the sea surface. They block out the light so plankton, which is at the beginning of the food chain, cannot grow. And, if the toxic oil gets onto fish, birds and other animals, it can kill them.

If an oil slick washes ashore it can affect even more wildlife and massive clean-up operations are needed.

Fractional Distillation

Humans **exploit** (use to their own benefit) natural sources of crude oil to produce lots of useful products, e.g. petrol and diesel oil.

Crude oil is a mixture of many **hydrocarbons**. A hydrocarbon is a molecule that contains only **carbon** and **hydrogen** atoms.

Different hydrocarbons have different boiling points. This means that crude oil can be separated into **fractions** (parts) by **heating** it in a process called **fractional distillation**.

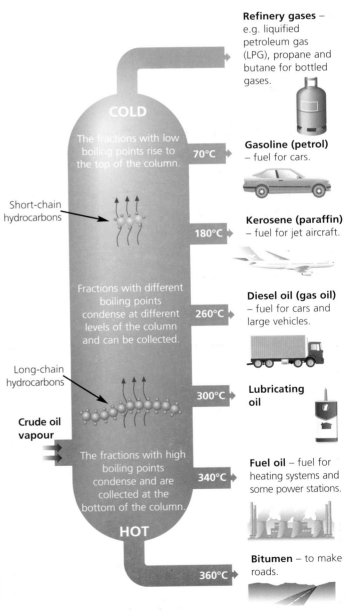

Refinery gases – e.g. liquified petroleum gas (LPG), propane and butane for bottled gases.

COLD
The fractions with low boiling points rise to the top of the column.

70°C

Gasoline (petrol) – fuel for cars.

Short-chain hydrocarbons

180°C

Kerosene (paraffin) – fuel for jet aircraft.

Fractions with different boiling points condense at different levels of the column and can be collected.

260°C

Diesel oil (gas oil) – fuel for cars and large vehicles.

Long-chain hydrocarbons

300°C

Lubricating oil

Crude oil vapour

The fractions with high boiling points condense and are collected at the bottom of the column.

340°C

Fuel oil – fuel for heating systems and some power stations.

HOT

360°C

Bitumen – to make roads.

Making Crude Oil Useful

Forces Between Molecules

The **atoms** in a hydrocarbon molecule are strongly held together by the bonds between them, for example...

Sometimes drawn as

Chemical reactions are needed to break these bonds.

Strong bonds

All hydrocarbon molecules have forces of attraction between them, but they are only weak. Chemists call these **intermolecular** forces. However, the longer the hydrocarbon molecule is, the greater the area it has 'in contact' with its neighbours and the stronger the intermolecular forces are, for example...

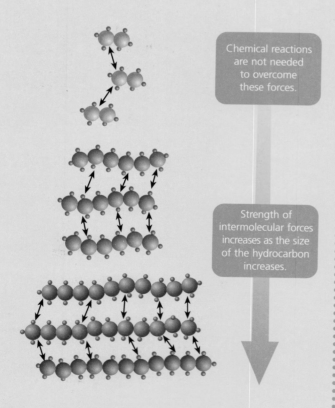

Chemical reactions are not needed to overcome these forces.

Strength of intermolecular forces increases as the size of the hydrocarbon increases.

The bonds between the carbon and hydrogen atoms within a hydrocarbon are stronger than the forces between hydrocarbon molecules.

Separating Hydrocarbons

When we heat a hydrocarbon its molecules move faster and faster until the intermolecular forces are broken.

Small molecules have very small forces of attraction between them and are easy to break by heating. This means that hydrocarbons with small molecules are volatile liquids or gases with low boiling points, for example...

- methane, CH_4, has a boiling point of -164°C
- ethane, C_2H_6, has a boiling point of -89°C.

Small molecule hydrocarbons

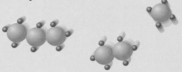

Large molecules have many more of these small forces between them, resulting in an overall large force of attraction. This force is more difficult to break by heating and hydrocarbons with large molecules are thick, viscous liquids or waxy solids with higher boiling points, for example...

- octane, C_8H_{18} has a boiling point of -126°C
- decane, $C_{10}H_{22}$ has a boiling point of -174°C.

Large molecule hydrocarbons

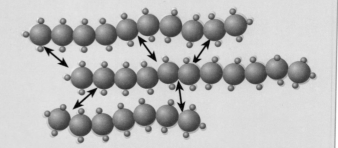

It is the differences in their boiling points which enable us to separate a mix of hydrocarbons (e.g. crude oil) by the process of fractional distillation.

The Fractions

Each fraction consists of a mixture of hydrocarbons whose boiling points fall within a particular **range**.

This table shows the main fractions obtained through the industrial fractional distillation of crude oil and their approximate boiling ranges.

Fraction	Boiling Range
Refinery gases	up to 25°C
Petrol	40–100°C
Kerosene	150–250°C
Diesel	220–350°C
Lubricating oil	over 350°C
Fuel oil	over 400°C
Bitumen	over 400°C

Cracking

Hydrocarbon molecules can be described as alkanes or alkenes, depending on whether or not they have a double bond present (see p.34).

Cracking converts **large alkane** molecules into **smaller**, **more useful**, **alkane** and **alkene** molecules. The alkene molecules obtained can be used to make polymers, which have many uses (see p.34–35). A typical example is the cracking of **naphtha** (the fraction which includes petrol) to obtain **petrol**.

To take place, cracking needs a **catalyst** and a **high temperature**. In the laboratory, cracking is carried out using the apparatus shown below.

Long-chain hydrocarbon   heat catalyst   Short-chain hydrocarbons

HT There is not enough petrol in crude oil to meet demand. Therefore, cracking is used to convert parts of crude oil that cannot be used into additional petrol.

Crude oil is found in many parts of the world, so oil companies have to work with lots of different countries to extract the oil. Oil is a very valuable resource and is often in the news as a source of conflict between nations and a target for terrorists.

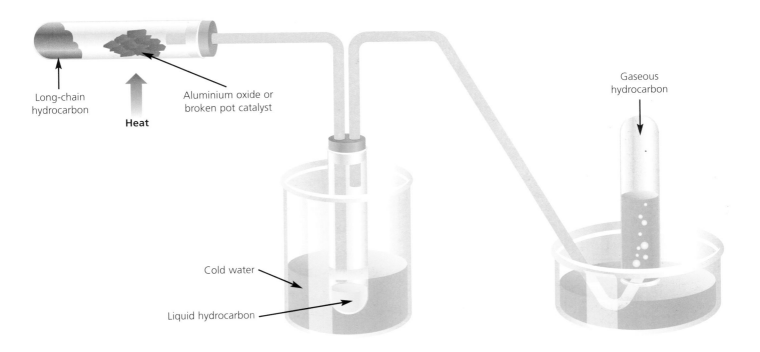

Long-chain hydrocarbon

Heat

Aluminium oxide or broken pot catalyst

Gaseous hydrocarbon

Cold water

Liquid hydrocarbon

Making Polymers

Hydrocarbons

You need to remember that…
- carbon atoms can make four bonds each
- hydrogen atoms can make one bond each

The start of a compound's name tells you what it contains…
- **meth**… contains one carbon atom
- **eth**… contains two carbon atoms
- **prop**… contains three carbon atoms
- **but**… contains four carbon atoms.

Alkanes

When the spine of a hydrocarbon contains **single covalent bonds** only, it is known as an **alkane**. The simplest alkane, methane, is made up of four hydrogen atoms and one carbon atom.

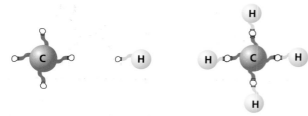

The name of an alkane always ends in **-ane**. This table shows the displayed and molecular formulae for the first four members of the alkane series.

Alkane	Displayed Formula	Molecular Formula
Methane	H | H − C − H | H	CH_4
Ethane	H H | | H − C − C − H | | H H	C_2H_6
Propane	H H H | | | H − C − C − C − H | | | H H H	C_3H_8
Butane	H H H H | | | | H − C − C − C − C − H | | | | H H H H	C_4H_{10}

Alkenes

The **alkenes** are another form of hydrocarbon. They are very similar to the alkanes except that they contain **one double covalent bond** between two adjacent carbon atoms. The simplest alkene is ethene, C_2H_4, which is made of…
- two carbon atoms
- four hydrogen atoms.

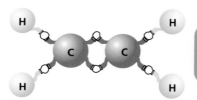

As you can see, ethene contains one double covalent bond between carbon atoms.

The name of an alkene always ends in **-ene**. The following table shows the displayed and molecular formulae for the first three members of the alkene series.

Alkene	Displayed Formula	Molecular Formula
Ethene	H H \ / C = C / \ H H	C_2H_4
Propene	H H \ | C = C − C − H / | | H H H	C_3H_6
Butene	H H H \ | | C = C − C − C − H / | | | H H H H	C_4H_8

Polymerisation

The alkenes made by cracking can be used as **monomers**, which can be reacted together to produce **polymers**. These are long-chain molecules, some of which make up plastics.

Alkenes are very good at joining together, and when they do so without producing another substance we call it **polymerisation**. This process, e.g. the formation of poly(ethene) from ethene, requires **high pressure** and a **catalyst**.

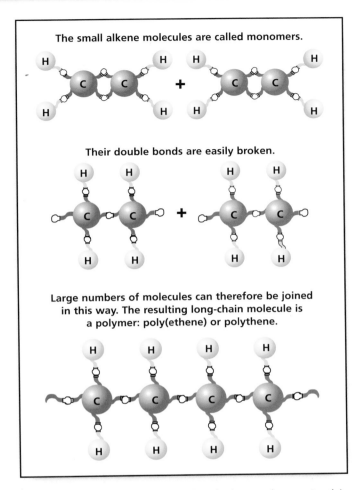

The small alkene molecules are called monomers.

Their double bonds are easily broken.

Large numbers of molecules can therefore be joined in this way. The resulting long-chain molecule is a polymer: poly(ethene) or polythene.

The resulting long-chain molecule is a polymer. In this case poly(ethene) – often called polythene – is formed.

Consider the displayed formula of ethene and poly(ethene)…

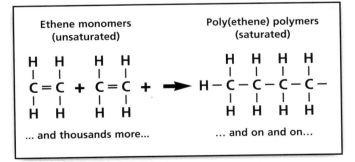

Ethene monomers (unsaturated)	Poly(ethene) polymers (saturated)

… and thousands more…   … and on and on…

A more compact way of writing this reaction uses the standard way of displaying a polymer formula.

Polymerisation involves the reaction of many unsaturated monomer molecules, i.e. alkenes, to form a saturated polymer. You will be expected to be able to construct the displayed formula of…

- a **polymer** given the displayed formula of a monomer, e.g. propene monomer to poly(propene) polymer

- a **monomer** given the displayed formula of a polymer, e.g poly(propene) polymer to propene monomer.

HT Hydrogen atoms react with carbon atoms to form a covalent bond. When this happens, carbon atoms share an electron pair with hydrogen atoms in order to bond.

Alkanes contain only single covalent bonds between the carbon atoms – they are described as **saturated** hydrocarbons. (They have the maximum number of hydrogen atoms per carbon atom in the molecule.)

Alkenes contain at least one double covalent bond, which means that two pairs of electrons are being shared between two atoms. This means that the carbon atom is not bonded to the maximum number of hydrogen atoms. Alkenes are therefore described as being **unsaturated**.

A simple test to distinguish between alkenes and alkanes is that alkenes will decolourise bromine water as the alkene reacts with it. Alkanes have no effect on bromine water.

Designer Polymers

Polymers

Polymers (plastics) have many properties that make them useful. You should be able to use these terms to explain why a certain plastic is used for a particular job. Properties include…

- easily moulded into shape
- waterproof
- electrical insulator
- non-biodegradable
- lightweight
- flexible
- can be printed on
- unreactive
- can be coloured
- heat insulator
- transparent
- tough.

Uses for Polymers

Different plastics have different properties which results in them having different uses…

Polymer	Properties	Uses
Polythene or poly(ethene)	• Light. • Flexible. • Easily moulded.	• Plastic bags. • Moulded containers.
Polystyrene	• Light. • Poor conductor of heat.	• Insulation and packaging (when expanded as foam).
Nylon	• Lightweight. • Waterproof. • Tough.	• Clothing. • Climbing ropes.
Polyester	• Lightweight. • Waterproof. • Tough.	• Clothing. • Bottles.

Outdoor Clothing

Outdoor clothing, such as a jacket, needs to be waterproof to keep the wearer dry. Nylon is an excellent material to use to make outdoor clothing because it is…

- lightweight
- tough
- waterproof (but it does not let water vapour escape, so it could be uncomfortable to wear if the wearer became hot and started to perspire)
- blocks UV light (harmful sunlight).

Gore-Tex®

Gore-Tex® is a breathable material made from nylon. It has all of the advantages of nylon, but it is also treated with a material that allows perspiration (water vapour) to escape whilst preventing rain from getting in. This is far more comfortable for people who lead an active outdoor life, as it prevents them from getting wet when they perspire.

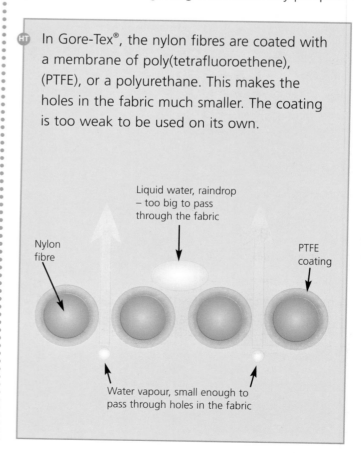

HT In Gore-Tex®, the nylon fibres are coated with a membrane of poly(tetrafluoroethene), (PTFE), or a polyurethane. This makes the holes in the fabric much smaller. The coating is too weak to be used on its own.

Liquid water, raindrop – too big to pass through the fabric

Nylon fibre

PTFE coating

Water vapour, small enough to pass through holes in the fabric

Designer Polymers

Structure of Plastics

Polymers (plastics), such as PVC, consist of a tangled mass of very long chain molecules, in which the atoms are held together by strong covalent bonds. The properties of a plastic depend on its structure.

Plastics that have weak forces between polymer molecules have low melting points and can be stretched easily as the polymer molecules can slide over one another.

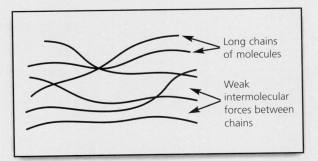

Long chains of molecules

Weak intermolecular forces between chains

Plastics that have strong forces between the polymer molecules (covalent bonds or cross-linking bridges) have high melting points, are rigid and cannot be stretched.

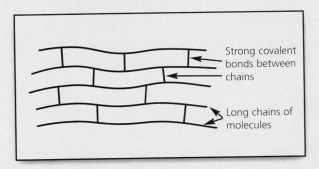

Strong covalent bonds between chains

Long chains of molecules

Disposal of Plastics

Research is being carried out on the development of biodegradable plastics to help reduce the impact that disposing of plastics has on the environment.

As we have seen, plastics have many different uses. As it is such a convenient material, we produce a large amount of plastic waste. This can be difficult to dispose of and can sometimes be seen as litter in the streets. There are various ways of disposing of plastics, unfortunately, some of them have a negative impact on the environment.

- Using **landfill sites** is a problem because most plastics are non-biodegradable. This means microorganisms have no effect on them and they will not decompose and rot away. Throwing plastics into landfill sites results in the waste of a valuable resource and, because of the volume of waste produced, landfill sites get filled up very quickly, which is also a waste of land.
- **Burning** plastics produces air pollution and also wastes valuable resources. The production of carbon dioxide contributes to the greenhouse effect which results in global warming. Some plastics cannot be burned at all as they produce toxic fumes. For example, burning poly(chloroethene) or PVC as it is more commonly known, produces hydrogen chloride gas.
- **Recycling** plastics is an option which prevents resources being wasted. However, different types of plastic need to be recycled separately. Sorting them into groups to be recycled can be difficult and very time-consuming.

Using Carbon Fuels

Choosing a Fuel

Some or all of the following factors should be taken into account when choosing a fuel for a specific purpose:

- energy value – how much energy do you get from a measured amount of fuel?
- availability – is the fuel easy to obtain?
- storage – how easy is it to store the fuel? (e.g. petrol is more difficult to store than coal)
- cost – how much fuel do you get for your money?
- toxicity – is the fuel (or its combustion products) poisonous?
- pollution – do the combustion products pollute the atmosphere?
- ease of use – is it easy to control and is special equipment needed?

Burning Fuels (Combustion)

When fuels burn, energy is released as heat. Chemists call this **combustion**. Many fuels are hydrocarbons. When fuels burn they react with the oxygen in the air. Reactions with oxygen (oxidation) produce **oxides**.

← Clean blue flame

← Air hole open

When a hydrocarbon, like methane, is burnt in air, only carbon dioxide and water (hydrogen oxide) are formed.

Methane	+	Oxygen	→	Carbon dioxide	+	Water

$$CH_{4(g)} + 2O_{2(g)} \longrightarrow CO_{2(g)} + 2H_2O_{(l)}$$

Evaluating a Fuel

Choosing a fuel to use for a particular job requires a careful study of available information.

In your exam you may be asked to evaluate the use of different fossil fuels using given data, e.g. tables, graphs, pie charts. The following are examples of the sort of fuels that might be considered.

Methane (CH_4)

- Colourless gas.
- Burns to form carbon dioxide and water.
- Non-toxic (but it is a greenhouse gas).
- Readily available through normal gas supplies.
- Not easy to store.
- 1 gram of methane produces 55.6kJ of energy when completely burned.

Butane (C_4H_{10})

- Easier to store and carry about than methane.
- Burns in the same way as methane.
- Used as camping gas.
- Only 26.9kJ of energy is produced from 1 gram when it is burned.

Coal

- Easy to store.
- Readily available, not very expensive and releases quite a lot of energy when burned.
- Main problem is pollution and in particular the sulfur dioxide gas (that leads to acid rain) it produces, along with smoke and other pollutants.
- Most major populated areas of the UK allow only smokeless coal to be burned as a fuel.

As the world's population increases and more countries become industrialised, the demand for fossil fuels continues to grow.

Using Carbon Fuels

Detecting the Products of Combustion

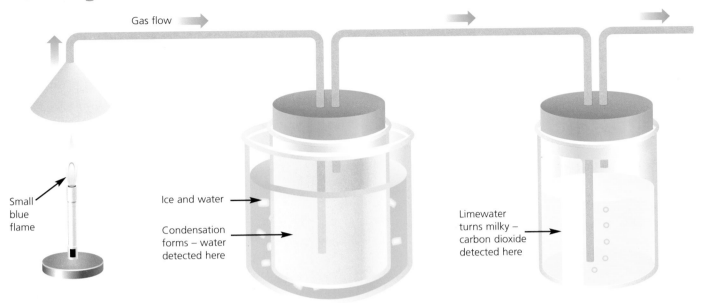

Gas flow →

Small blue flame

Ice and water

Condensation forms – water detected here

Limewater turns milky – carbon dioxide detected here

Incomplete Combustion

If a fuel burns without sufficient oxygen, e.g. in a room with poor ventilation or when a gas appliance needs servicing, then **incomplete combustion** takes place and **carbon monoxide** (a poisonous gas) can be formed. For example, the incomplete combustion of methane…

Methane	**+**	Oxygen	→	Carbon monoxide	**+**	Water
HT $2CH_{4(g)}$	**+**	$3O_{2(g)}$	→	$2CO_{(g)}$	**+**	$4H_2O_{(l)}$

If there is **very little oxygen** available, **carbon** is produced instead. For example, the burning of methane when very little oxygen is available…

Methane	**+**	Oxygen	→	Carbon	**+**	Water
HT $CH_{4(g)}$	**+**	$O_{2(g)}$	→	$C_{(s)}$	**+**	$2H_2O_{(l)}$

Although incomplete combustion does release energy, much more is released when complete combustion takes place. Other advantages in making sure a fuel burns completely include…

- less soot is produced
- no poisonous carbon monoxide gas is produced.

Gas appliances should be serviced regularly to make sure that they are operating efficiently. If they are faulty, they will not burn completely and poisonous carbon monoxide will be released.

A blue flame on a Bunsen burner transfers more energy than a yellow flame because it involves complete combustion. The yellow flame shows incomplete combustion is taking place.

You should now be able to write the word equations for complete and incomplete combustion if you are given the formula of the fuel, but remember…

- oxygen is diatomic – its atoms are only ever found in pairs: O_2
- complete combustion of a hydrocarbon produces water and carbon dioxide
- incomplete combustion of a hydrocarbon produces water and carbon monoxide
- incomplete combustion when there is only a small amount of oxygen produces water and carbon.

Energy

Exothermic and Endothermic Reactions

Many reactions are accompanied by a **temperature rise**. These are known as **exothermic** reactions because heat energy is **given out** to the surroundings.

Some reactions are accompanied by a **fall in temperature**. These reactions are known as **endothermic** reactions because heat energy is **taken in** from the surroundings (the reaction absorbs energy).

Useful Energy

Chemical reactions can be used to…
- heat things, e.g. combustion of methane (natural gas) using Bunsen burner
- produce electricity
- make sound, e.g. in a firework
- make light, e.g. burning magnesium in air.

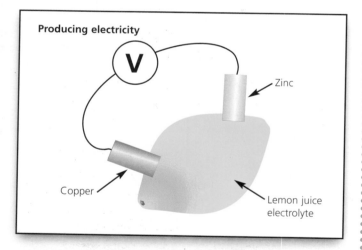

Producing electricity
V
Zinc
Copper
Lemon juice electrolyte

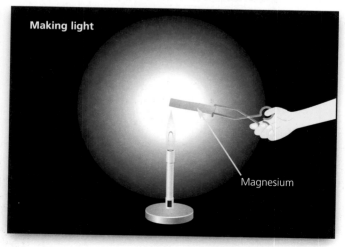

Making light
Magnesium

Comparing Fuels

The equipment shown in the diagram below can be used to compare the amounts of heat energy released by the combustion of different fuels. The greater the rise in the temperature of the water, the greater the amount of energy produced in joules (J) or kilojoules (kJ) released from the fuel being used.

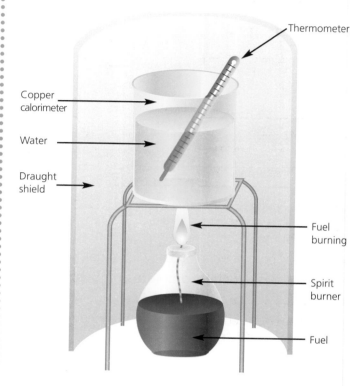

Thermometer
Copper calorimeter
Water
Draught shield
Fuel burning
Spirit burner
Fuel

To make meaningful comparisons we would need to carry out a **fair test** each time. We would need to…
- use the same mass (volume) of water
- use the same calorimeter
- have the burner and calorimeter the same distance apart
- burn the same mass of fuel for the same length of time.

The formula used to work out the change in temperature (°C) is…

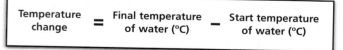

| Temperature change | = | Final temperature of water (°C) | − | Start temperature of water (°C) |

If you burn the same mass of each fuel, the fuel that produces the largest temperature rise releases the most energy.

Breaking and Making Bonds

Bottled gas (propane) burns in air to release lots of energy.

In displayed formula, the equation for the burning of propane looks like this…

```
    H   H   H                    O = O
    |   |   |                    O = O
H — C — C — C — H     +          O = O
    |   |   |                    O = O
    H   H   H                    O = O
```

All the bonds in propane and oxygen have to be broken. Energy needs to be taken in to break the bonds.

▼

```
    O       O
   / \     / \                   O = C = O
  H   H   H   H         +        O = C = O
    O       O                    O = C = O
   / \     / \
  H   H   H   H
```

All the bonds in water and carbon dioxide have to be made. Energy is given out when bonds are made.

When propane burns, more energy is given out when the new bonds are made than is taken in to break the old bonds at the start. The **overall energy change** is exothermic.

If more energy has to be taken in to break the old bonds at the start of the reaction than is given out when new bonds are made, then the overall reaction is endothermic.

Calculating Energy Changes

In order to compare fuels, we would need to work out the amount of energy transferred by the fuel to the water, and the amount of energy transferred per gram of fuel burned. The results from an experiment with hexane are as follows.

	Start	End
Mass of burner and hexane	187.60g	187.34g
Temperature of water	22°C	34°C

Mass of hexane burned
$(187.60 - 187.34)$ = **0.26g**

Rise in temperature of water = **12°C**

Mass of water in calorimeter = **200g**

The amount of energy transferred to the water can be calculated by using the following formula…

$$\text{Energy supplied to raise energy} \longrightarrow \text{Mass} \times \text{Specific heat capacity} \times \text{Temperature change}$$

Energy supplied = 200g x 4.2J/g°C x 12°C
= **10 080 joules**

N.B. Specific heat capacity is a constant that is specific to a particular liquid. For water it has a value of 4.2J/g°C.

We can now work out the energy transferred per gram of fuel burned using the following formula…

$$\text{Energy per gram} = \frac{\text{Energy supplied}}{\text{Mass of fuel burnt}}$$

Energy per gram = $\dfrac{10\,080J}{0.26g}$
= **38 769J/g**

The actual value for hexane is 48 407J/g. Our result is lower because not all the energy is transferred to the water. Some is lost to the surroundings and some is transferred to the copper calorimeter causing its temperature to rise.

You will need to recall both of the above formulae.

Heating Houses

Heat Flow

Every year we spend millions of pounds heating our houses but much of this heat energy escapes through our windows and roofs. We can use our understanding of temperature and heat flow to help us to reduce our energy usage and save us money.

Thermograms

Temperature can be represented by a range of colours in a thermogram. In this example…

- the windows are where most heat energy is escaping so they show up as yellow
- the well-insulated loft is where the least heat energy is escaping so this shows up as purple.

Temperature

Temperature is a measure of how hot something is. The unit of measurement is **degrees Celsius, °C**.

Heat is a measurement of **energy** and is measured in **joules, J**.

> **HT** **Temperature** is a measurement of how **hot** something is using a **chosen scale**, usually **degrees Celsius, °C** (but sometimes Fahrenheit, °F).
>
> **Heat** is a measurement of **energy** on an **absolute scale**, always **joules, J**.

If there is a **difference in temperature** between an object and its surroundings then this results in the **flow of heat energy** from the **hotter** region to the **cooler** region.

If an object's **temperature rises** it is **taking in heat energy**. For example, if you take a can of cola out of the fridge it will soon warm up to room temperature because the can takes in heat energy from the air in the room.

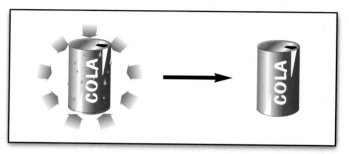

If an object's **temperature falls** it is **giving out heat energy**. For example, a hot cup of tea will soon cool down. If you hold it in your hands you will feel the heat energy flowing from the cup into your hands.

When an object has a **very high temperature** it will **cool down very quickly**. As its temperature drops, it will cool down at a slower rate.

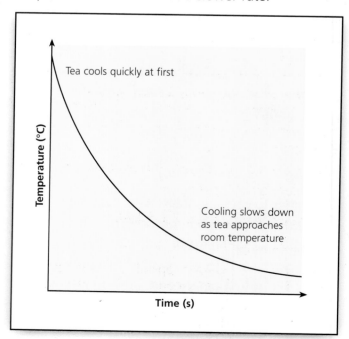

Tea cools quickly at first

Cooling slows down as tea approaches room temperature

Temperature (°C)

Time (s)

Measuring Heat Energy

The amount of energy needed to raise the temperature of an object depends on…

- the **mass** of the object
- the **change in temperature** required
- the **specific heat capacity** (see opposite) of the material that the object is made from.

The experiment below measures the amount of heat energy required to change the temperature of an aluminium block.

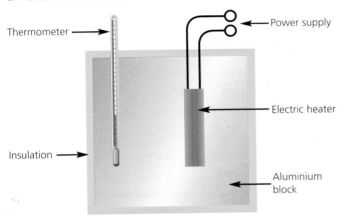

Thermometer

Power supply

Electric heater

Insulation

Aluminium block

The electric heater provides 100J of heat energy per second, i.e. every second, 100J of heat energy passes into the aluminum.

Therefore, if you time how many seconds it takes for the temperature of the aluminium to rise by a certain amount, e.g. 10°C, you can calculate the amount of energy used to bring about the change using this formula...

| Total energy supplied | = | Energy supplied per second | **X** | Number of seconds |

Example

It takes 50 seconds to raise the temperature of the aluminium block by 10°C.

Calculate the total energy supplied.

Use the formula…

$$\text{Total energy supplied} = \text{Energy supplied per second} \times \text{Number of seconds}$$

$$= 100\text{J/s} \times 50\text{s}$$

$$= \textbf{5000J}$$

Specific Heat Capacity

Specific heat capacity is the energy needed to raise the temperature of **1kg** of material by **1°C**.

Each material has its **own value**, which is a measure of how much energy it can hold.

HT The following equation is used to find the amount of energy required to raise the temperature of an object by a certain amount.

| Energy (J) | = | Mass (kg) | **X** | Specific heat capacity (J/kg°C) | **X** | Temperature change (°C) |

Example 1

The specific heat capacity of copper is 387J/kg°C.

Calculate how much heat energy is required to raise the temperature of a 5kg block of copper by 10°C.

Use the formula…

$$\text{Energy} = \text{Mass} \times \frac{\text{Specific heat}}{\text{capacity}} \times \frac{\text{Temperature}}{\text{change}}$$

$$= 5\text{kg} \times 387\text{J/kg°C} \times 10\text{°C}$$

$$= \textbf{19 350J}$$

Example 2

It takes 28 800J of heat energy to raise the temperature of a 4kg block of aluminium by 8°C. Calculate the specific heat capacity of aluminium.

Rearrange the formula…

$$\frac{\text{Specific}}{\text{heat}} = \frac{\text{Energy}}{\text{Mass} \times \text{Temperature change}}$$

$$= \frac{28\,800}{4 \times 8}$$

$$= \textbf{900J/kg°C}$$

Heating Houses

Melting and Boiling

The data below shows how the temperature of the water in a kettle changed with time.

Time (s)	0	30	60	90	120	150
Temperature (°C)	21	39	55	68	79	88
Time (s)	180	210	240	270	300	
Temperature (°C)	95	100	100	100	100	

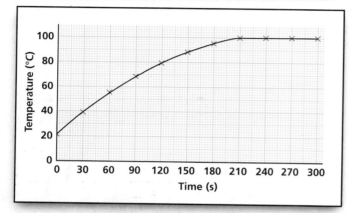

The temperature rises sharply to begin with but once it hits 100°C it stops rising. It remains **constant**.

The temperature of the **water** will never rise above **100°C**, no matter how long it is heated for. This is because when the water reaches 100°C, all the **heat energy** supplied by the kettle is being used to **boil** the water.

Likewise, when you put **ice** in a drink, it does not melt immediately because it requires **energy to melt**.

The temperature of a material does not change when it is at the point of **boiling**, **melting** or **freezing** (i.e. changing state). So, to **interpret data** which shows the heating or cooling of an object, look for places where the temperature stays the same.

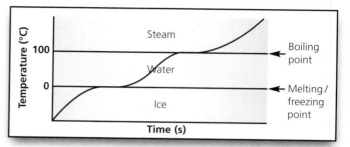

HT During the melting and boiling of water, the energy supplied is used to break **inter-molecular bonds** as the water molecules change state, from solid to liquid and from liquid to gas. This explains why the temperature of the material does not change.

Specific Latent Heat

The amount of heat energy required to melt or boil 1kg of a material is called the **specific latent heat**. It depends on...

- the **material**
- the **state** (solid, liquid or gas).

HT The energy required to boil or melt a certain mass of a material can be found with the following equation.

Energy (J) = Mass (kg) X Specific latent heat (J/kg)

Example
The **specific latent heat** of ice is 330 000J/kg. An ice sculpture with a mass of 10kg is left to melt on a hot day. Calculate the amount of energy required to melt the ice.

Using the equation...
Energy = Mass x Specific latent heat
= 10 x 330 000
= **3 300 000J**

Conductors and Insulators

Materials that allow energy to spread through them quickly are called **conductors**. **Metals** are good conductors.

Materials that allow energy to spread through them much more slowly are called **insulators**. Most **non-metals**, such as **wood**, **plastic**, **glass** and **air** are good insulators. Below are some everyday examples of conductors and insulators in action.

- A saucepan is made of a good conductor, e.g. copper or aluminium.
- A saucepan's handle is made of a good insulator, e.g. wood or plastic.
- Clothing and bedding are both good insulators, because they trap air within their material, and between the layers.
- Curtains are good insulators and they also trap a layer of air between them and the window which helps reduce energy loss.

Reducing Heat Losses in the Home

Apart from curtains, there are many different ways in which heat losses from a home can be reduced. An important consideration with all of them is the **payback time**. This is how long it takes to pay for the insulation from the savings made.

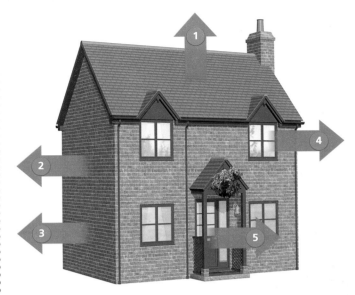

1 Fibreglass Roof Insulation	
Cost	£400
Annual saving	£80
Payback time	5 years
2 Reflective Foil on or in Walls	
Cost	£40
Annual saving	£10
Payback time	4 years
3 Cavity Wall Insulation	
Cost	£600
Annual saving	£30
Payback time	20 years
4 Double Glazing	
Cost	£1800
Annual saving	£60
Payback time	30 years
5 Draught Excluders	
Cost	£40
Annual saving	£20
Payback time	2 years

Keeping Homes Warm

Saving Energy in the Home

Each design feature in the house on the previous page helps to save energy by reducing heat loss. The table below explains how.

Method of Insulation	Reduces...	How?
Fibreglass roof insulation	• Conduction. • Convection.	• By trapping layers of air (a good insulator) between the fibres.
Reflective foil on walls	• Radiation.	• By reflecting heat energy back into the room.
Cavity wall insulation	• Conduction. • Convection.	• By trapping air in the foam.
Double glazing	• Conduction. • Convection.	• By trapping air between the panes of glass.
Draught excluders	• Convection.	• By keeping as much warm air inside as possible.

Other Examples

- Kettles made of metal have shiny surfaces to reduce heat loss by **radiation**.
- A hot-water tank is made of stainless steel which reduces heat loss by **radiation**. It may also have a shiny outer layer to reduce heat loss by radiation. Hot water tanks usually have an insulating jacket, again to reduce heat loss by conduction and convection.
- Refrigerators are insulated to reduce heat gain by **conduction** and **convection**.

Energy Efficiency

Energy efficiency is a measure of how good an appliance is at converting input energy into **useful** output energy.

For a television, the input energy is electrical energy and the useful energy output is light and sound. We need to be able to see and hear the programmes. But televisions also produce heat energy which in this case is a waste energy.

The equation we use to calculate efficiency is:

$$\text{Efficiency (no unit)} = \frac{\text{Useful output energy (J)}}{\text{Total energy input (J)}}$$

Example

A 60 watt light bulb uses 60 joules of energy every second. In 50 seconds it gives out 300 joules of light energy. Use the formula to calculate the efficiency of the light bulb.

$$\text{Efficiency} = \frac{\text{Useful output energy}}{\text{Total energy input}}$$

$$= \frac{300}{60 \times 50}$$

$$= 0.1 \times 100 = \textbf{10\%}$$

Multiply by 100 to get a percentage

Transfer of Heat Energy

Heat energy does not stay in one place; it moves around. It can be transferred from one place to another in three ways: conduction, convection and radiation.

HT Conduction

This is the transfer of heat energy through a substance from the hotter region to the cooler region without any movement of the substance itself.

As a substance, i.e. the metal poker, is heated, the kinetic energy of the particles increases. This kinetic energy is transferred between the particles in the poker and gradually energy is transferred along the substance.

Convection

Since fluids (liquids) and gases can flow they can transfer heat energy from hotter to cooler regions by their own movement.

As the liquid or gas gets hotter, its particles move faster, causing it to expand and become less dense. It will now rise up and be replaced by colder, denser liquid or gas.

Example 1

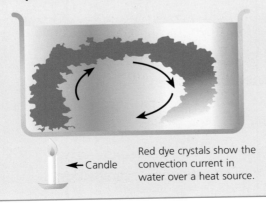

← Candle

Red dye crystals show the convection current in water over a heat source.

Example 2

Circulation of air caused by a radiator

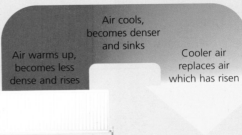

Air cools, becomes denser and sinks

Air warms up, becomes less dense and rises

Cooler air replaces air which has risen

Radiation

This is the transfer of heat energy by waves. Hot objects emit mainly infrared radiation which can pass through a vacuum, i.e. no medium is needed for its transfer. How much radiation is given out or taken in by an object depends on its surface.

Dark matt surfaces emit more radiation than light shiny surfaces at the same temperature.

5 mins later

5 mins later

Dark matt surfaces are better absorbers (poorer reflectors) of radiation than light shiny surfaces at the same temperature.

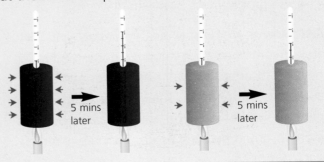

5 mins later

5 mins later

Cooking with Waves

The Electromagnetic Spectrum

Light is a part of the electromagnetic spectrum.

Together with the other forms of radiation, it makes a continuous spectrum which extends beyond each end of the visible spectrum produced by light.

Each type of electromagnetic radiation…

- travels at the same speed through space (a vacuum) – 300 000 000m/s
- has a different wavelength and a different frequency.

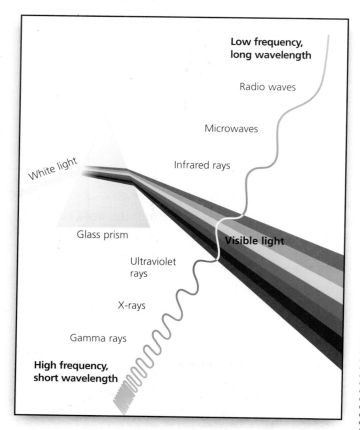

Uses of Electromagnetic Radiation

Radio waves are used to transmit radio and television programmes between places.

Microwaves are used to heat materials, and for satellite communication, mobile phones and radar. They are absorbed by water molecules, which causes them to heat up. They can penetrate about 1cm into food or into **you** and can cause burns when absorbed by body tissue. They are reflected by metal but can travel through glass and plastics.

Infrared rays are used to heat materials, and are used in cooking and in remote controls. In cooking, they are used to heat the surface of the food. They are absorbed by black objects, and reflected off shiny surfaces.

Visible light is used to carry information via optical fibres.

X-rays can be used to produce shadow images of bones to be used for medical diagnosis.

Gamma rays can be used in medical treatments.

Dangers of Electromagnetic Radiation

Ultraviolet light can cause sunburn and damage living cells.

Microwaves are emitted from mobile phones. There are some concerns that these microwaves could have a detrimental impact on health, e.g. cause ear or brain tumours, brain damage or changes to DNA.

However, as yet there is no conclusive evidence of this.

A major concern is that if using mobile phones does affect our health, then children could be more at risk because they could be more susceptible to the microwave signals as a child's skull is not as thick as an adult's skull.

HT **Microwaves** are absorbed by water particles in the outside layers of the food, increasing the kinetic energy of the particles.

Energy is then transferred to the centre of the food by **conduction** or **convection**.

Infrared is absorbed by all of the particles on the surface of the food, increasing the kinetic energy of the particles.

Energy is then transferred to the centre of the food by **conduction** or **convection**.

Infrared Signals

Infrared radiation is one type of electromagnetic wave which, together with various other types such as visible light, forms the electromagnetic spectrum.

Infrared is used in many commonplace devices, e.g.

- the remote controls for your TV and video
- sensors that control automatic doors at the supermarket
- short-distance data links for computers or mobile phones
- burglar alarms (by detecting body heat)
- security lights (by detecting body heat).

Optical Fibres

An optical fibre is a long, flexible, transparent cable of very small diameter.

As **pulses** of light or **infrared** radiation travel down an optical fibre they are not refracted but **totally internally reflected** along its length because the glass–air boundary acts like a plane mirror. The same internal reflection occurs at water–air and Perspex–air boundaries. In this way, optical fibres allow the rapid transmission of data necessary for modern-day communications.

Refraction

Usually, when a ray of light or infrared passes from glass into air it is **refracted** away from the normal. This happens if the angle of incidence is below a certain value.

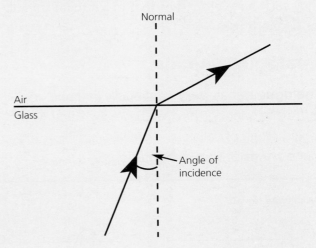

Reflection

However, if the angle of incidence is beyond a certain value the light or infrared is **totally internally reflected** and not refracted. This is what happens inside an optical fibre.

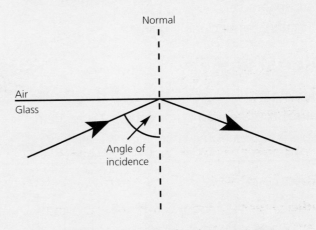

An optical fibre transfers light by totally internally reflecting it along its length.

Infrared Signals

Signals

There are two types of signal that can be used to transmit data. They are…

- analogue
- digital.

They each have properties that make them suitable for different uses.

Analogue Signals

Analogue signals **vary** continually in amplitude and / or frequency. They can have any value within a fixed range of values and are very similar to the sound waves of speech or music.

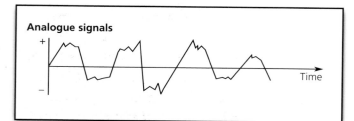

Examples of analogue devices include…

- dimmer switches
- thermometers
- speedometers
- meters that include a pointer.

Digital Signals

Digital signals do not vary; they have only **two values** or states: **on** (1) or **off** (0). There are no values in between. The information is a series of pulses.

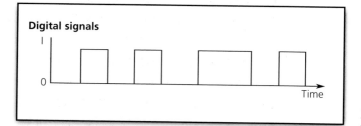

Examples of digital devices include…

- on / off switches
- digital meters
- digital clocks
- digital scales.

Analogue signals are like a dimmer switch, which can set lighting to variable levels rather than just on or off.

Digital signals are like an on-off switch, which has only two settings, on and off.

Advantages of Digital Signals

More information can be transmitted via optical fibres. Known as **multiplexing**, this is a technique where two or more digital signals can be carried down the same fibre.

Both digital and analogue signals suffer from interference in the form of **noise** but this is easily removable from digital signals leaving them as clear as when they were first sent.

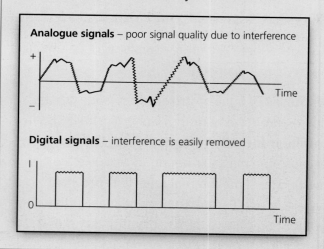

Wireless Signals

Electromagnetic radiation (such as radio waves and microwaves) can be used to send information without optical fibres because it can be reflected and refracted in the same way as visible light (see p.49). This **wireless technology** is used in **radios**, **mobile phones** and **laptop** computers and has three main advantages:

- signals are available 24 hours a day
- no wiring is needed
- enables items to be portable and convenient.

Radio Waves

Radio waves are used for **satellite communication** and to transmit **radio** and **television programmes** around the world. Some radio signals are better quality than others because radio stations with similar transmission frequencies often interfere with one another (see p.52).

Microwaves

Mobile phones use microwave signals but they are not the same wavelength as those used in microwave cookers.

However, there is public concern about children using mobile phones and the possible dangers to users and people who live near transmission masts.

Microwaves are used to transmit information over large distances that are in **line of sight**. Some areas are not in line of sight so they have poor signals, which is why your mobile phone may cut out or fail to get a connection (see diagram below).

Transmitting Signals

Satellites can be used for global communication. A signal is sent from a ground station transmitter dish to a satellite receiver dish. A return signal is then sent by the satellite transmitter to a ground receiver dish, which may be in a different country, continent, etc.

The **ionosphere** is an electrically charged layer in the Earth's upper atmosphere. **Longer wavelength** radio waves are **reflected** by the ionosphere. This enables radio and television programmes to be transmitted between different places, which may be in different countries, continents, etc.

The refraction and diffraction of radiation can affect communications:

- refraction at the interfaces of different layers of the Earth's atmosphere results in the waves changing direction
- diffraction (changes to the direction and intensity of waves) at the edge of transmission dishes causes the waves to spread out which results in signal loss.

Interference from similar signals limits the distance between transmitters. Positioning transmitters in high places can help to overcome the nuisance of obstacles blocking the signals.

Light

Light

Light is a **transverse wave**. The other type of wave, such as that produced when a tuning fork vibrates, is called **longitudinal**). A transverse wave can be demonstrated using a slinky spring or by tying one end of a rope to a wall (see below).

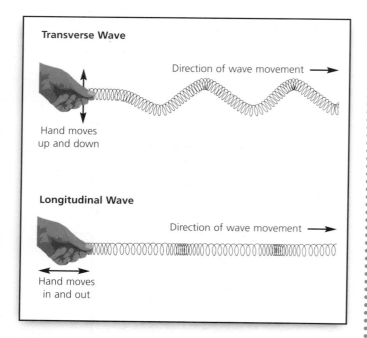

Light has some important features:

- **amplitude** – the maximum disturbance caused by the wave
- **wavelength** – the distance between corresponding points on two successive disturbances (i.e. from a peak to the next peak)
- **frequency** – the number of waves produced (or that pass a particular point) in one second.

The Wave Equation

The relationship between wave speed, frequency and wavelength is...

Wave speed (m/s) = Frequency (Hz) x Wavelength (m)

$$\frac{v}{f \times \lambda}$$

where v is wave speed, f is frequency and λ is wavelength.

However, all electromagnetic waves travel at the same speed in a vacuum (e.g. space).

Example

A tapped tuning fork of frequency 480Hz produces sound waves of wavelength 70cm. What is the speed of the sound wave?

Using our relationship...

Wave speed = Frequency x Wavelength
= 480Hz x 0.7m ← Wavelength must be in metres.
= **336m/s**

Example (HT)

Radio 5 Live transmits on a frequency of 909kHz. If the speed of radio waves is 300 000 000m/s, on what wavelength does it transmit?

Rearrange the formula...

$$\text{Wavelength} = \frac{\text{Wave speed}}{\text{Frequency}}$$

$$= \frac{300\,000\,000 \text{m/s}}{909\,000 \text{Hz}} = \textbf{330m}$$

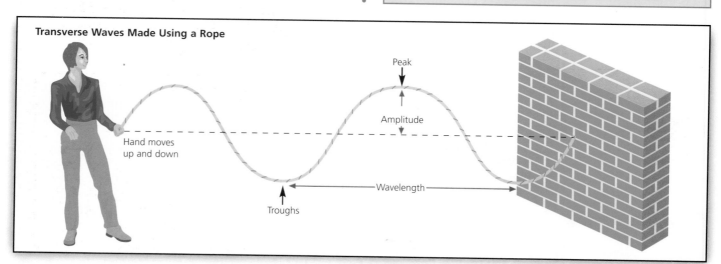

Transverse Waves Made Using a Rope

Hand moves up and down

Peak

Amplitude

Wavelength

Troughs

Light

Communicating with Light

Like all **electromagnetic waves**, light travels very fast. The reason why modern communication is so fast is because it uses light as a signal.

Today, optical fibres are used to carry signals in binary code but at the beginning of the last century, **Morse code** was used. Morse code replaces letters with a series of dots and dashes or short and long flashes of light.

P H Y S I C S

.--. .... -.-- ... .. -.-. ...

The light is produced by a **laser**, which produces a narrow, intense beam of light.

HT Lasers produce an intense beam of light in which all light waves are…

- the same frequency
- in phase with each other.

This means that all the peaks and troughs match up: they go up together and down together. When waves are in phase they have a lot of energy.

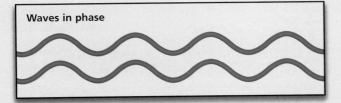

Waves in phase

Waves out of phase will have less overall energy.

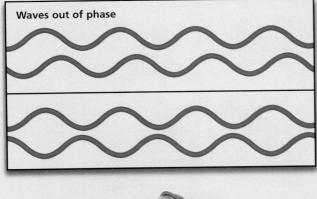

Waves out of phase

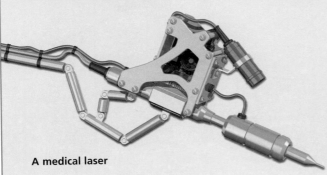

A medical laser

Compact Discs

Digital information can be stored as a sequence of tiny pits in a metal layer inside a compact disc (CD).

A CD player spins the disc and laser light is reflected from the pits. The reflected pulses of light are then turned into electrical signals on their way to the amplifier.

Using Signals

Light travels very fast and can be sent down optical cables via total internal reflection with only a very small amount of signal loss (see p.49). However, light is not used for wireless signalling as it does not diffract as well as radiowaves.

Electrical signals can be sent along wires, but the resistance of the wire causes the signal to deteriorate.

Radio waves diffract around obstacles making them ideal for wireless signalling, but diffraction can also lead to signal loss.

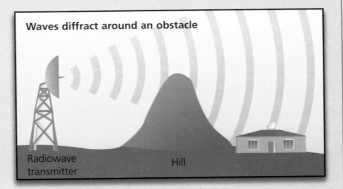

Waves diffract around an obstacle

Radiowave transmitter   Hill

Stable Earth

Earthquakes

Earthquakes produce shock waves which can travel inside the Earth and cause damage. These waves are called **seismic waves** and can be detected by seismometers. There are two types of seismic wave:

- **P-waves** (primary waves) are longitudinal and travel through both solids and liquids
- **S-waves** (secondary waves) are transverse waves (see p.52) and travel through solids but not through liquids. They travel slower than P-waves.

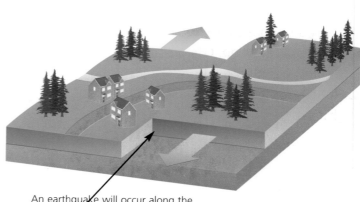

An earthquake will occur along the line where the two plates meet

HT The properties of seismic waves provide evidence for the structure of the Earth. After an earthquake occurs, the waves are detected all over the world as shown in the diagram. P-waves are able to travel through the liquid outer core so are detected in most places. S-waves will not pass through liquid so are only detected closer to the epicentre (the centre of the earthquake).

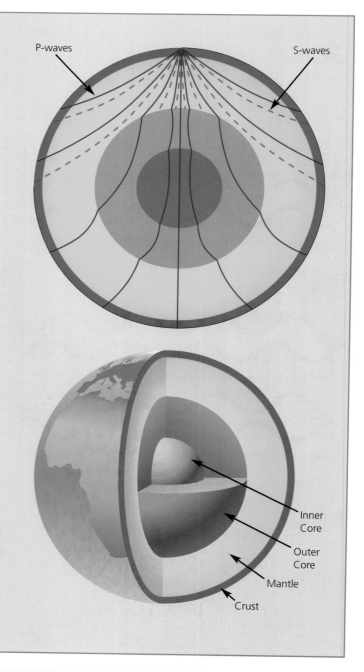

Primary Waves (P-waves) – occur first

Primary waves are longitudinal waves: the ground is made to vibrate in the same direction as the wave is travelling, i.e. up and down. They can travel through solids and liquids and through all layers of the Earth.

Secondary Waves (S-waves) – occur second

Secondary waves are transverse waves: the ground is made to vibrate at right angles to the direction the wave is travelling, i.e. from left to right. They can travel through solids but not liquids. They cannot travel through the Earth's outer core and are slower than primary waves.

A study of seismic waves indicates that the Earth is made up of…

- a thin crust
- a mantle which is semi-fluid and extends almost halfway to the centre
- a core which is over half of the Earth's diameter with a liquid outer part and a solid inner part.

Dangerous Sun

The Sun is responsible for life on Earth but it can also be very damaging. One kind of electromagnetic wave produced by the Sun is called **ultraviolet radiation** and prolonged exposure can cause **sunburn** or **skin cancer**.

People with darker skin are less at risk because their skin absorbs more ultraviolet radiation so less reaches the underlying body tissue.

Sun cream is also effective at reducing the damage caused by ultraviolet radiation. The higher the factor, the lower the risk because high factors allow longer exposure without burning. On a bright sunny day in England it is advised that you spend no more than 20 minutes in the midday sun. By wearing a factor 2 sun block you can double this time…

Safe time	=	Recommended exposure time	X	Sun block factor

Safe time = 20 minutes x 2
= **40 minutes**

Factor 3 will triple the time you can spend in the sun and so on. Factor 30 should keep you safe for 10 hours which should see you safely through a whole day as long as you keep reapplying it.

HT Global temperatures have increased by around 0.6°C since the late-19th century and by around 0.25°C over the past 25 years, which is the period with the most credible data. This warming has not been everywhere on the globe and some areas have, in fact, cooled over the last century. Nobody really knows for sure if the warming will continue at this rate, increase or slow down.

If the increase we have seen in the last 25 years continues then we would expect to see a 1°C increase in temperature by the end of this century. (100 years is 4 times longer than 25 years so the temperature change will be 4 times larger than 0.25°C.)

HT Ozone Depletion

Ozone is a gas found naturally high up in the Earth's atmosphere which prevents too many harmful ultraviolet (UV) rays reaching the Earth.

Recently, scientists have noticed that the ozone layer is becoming thinner and more people are suffering from skin cancer.

Many people blame the use of **CFCs** (chlorofluorocarbons) in factories, fridges and aerosol cans for this change in the ozone layer.

Ozone layer prevents some UV rays reaching the Earth

Global Warming

Many scientists believe that we are experiencing global warming which may have serious implications for the Earth in the near or distant future. Three contributing factors to global warming are…

- increased energy use both in homes and industry
- increased carbon dioxide (CO_2) emissions from fossil fuels
- deforestation, which is the cutting down of large numbers of trees.

Effect on Weather

Weather patterns are also affected by human activity, as well as by natural phenomena, e.g…

- dust from factories reflects radiation back into cities, causing warming
- dust from volcanoes reflects radiation from the Sun back into space, causing cooling.

Ecology in our School Grounds

Sampling Methods

A **population** is the total number of individuals of the same species that live in a certain area, e.g. the number of field mice in a meadow.

The size and distribution of a population can be measured by employing one or more of the following techniques:

Using Pooters

This is a simple technique in which insects are gathered up easily without harm. With this method, you get to find out what species are actually present, although you have to be systematic about your sampling in order to get representative results and it is difficult to get ideas of numbers.

A Pooter

Insects sucked in here

You suck here

Fine mesh to stop you from sucking the insects into your mouth

Using Sweepnets

These are employed in long grass or even moderately dense woodland where there are lots of shrubs. Again, it is difficult to get truly representative samples, particularly in terms of the relative numbers of organisms.

A Sweepnet

Using Pitfall Traps

These are set into the ground and used to catch small insects, e.g. beetles. Sometimes a mixture of ethanol and water is placed in the bottom of the trap to kill the samples, but there is no reason to do this. It is far better to just let the trapped insects go. This method can give an indication of the relative numbers of organisms in a given area.

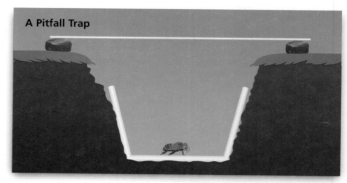

A Pitfall Trap

Using Quadrats

Quadrats are square frames that have sides of length 0.5m. They provide excellent results as long as they are thrown randomly. The population of a certain species can then be estimated. For example, if an average of 4 dandelion plants are found in each $0.25m^2$ quadrat, a scientist would estimate that 16 dandelion plants would be found in each $1m^2$, and 16 000 dandelion plants in a field if it is $1000m^2$.

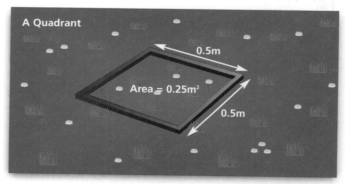

A Quadrant

0.5m

Area = $0.25m^2$

0.5m

HT When sampling, you must make sure you...
- take a big enough sample to make the results a good estimate – the larger the sample then the more accurate the results
- sample randomly – the more random the sample the more likely it is to be representative of the population.

Some Important Ecological Terms

The **habitat** of an animal or plant is its home – the part of the physical environment where it lives. An organism must be well-suited to its environment to be able to compete with other species for limited resources.

A **population** is the number of individuals of a species (see p.56).

A **community** is the total number of individuals of all the different populations of plant and animal living together in a habitat at any one time.

An **ecosystem** is a physical environment with a particular set of conditions, plus all the organisms which live in it.

Natural and Artificial Ecosystems

Natural ecosystems are not man-made (although they may be managed and preserved to provide good habitats for communities of plants and animals). They change over time. Examples of natural ecosystems are…
- woodlands
- ponds.

Artificial ecosystems are completely man-made and carefully controlled to keep the conditions constant. Examples of artificial ecosystems are…
- greenhouses
- fish farms.

> Natural ecosystems have high **biodiversity** – many different species of plants and animals coexist in the same environment.
>
> Artificial ecosystems are designed and maintained for a particular purpose. A market gardener growing a crop in a greenhouse uses **fertilisers**, **weedkillers** and **pesticides** to prevent other animals and plants from growing alongside his crop. The biodiversity in this ecosystem will be low.

Comparing Ecological Habitats

Two habitats can be compared by sampling using a quadrat. First the plant and animal species in a 1m² quadrat must be identified and then the population of each species must be counted. This process is repeated several times to get a large, reliable, random sample.

Correctly identifying species that you find in your sample can be tricky, so an identification key (see below) can help.

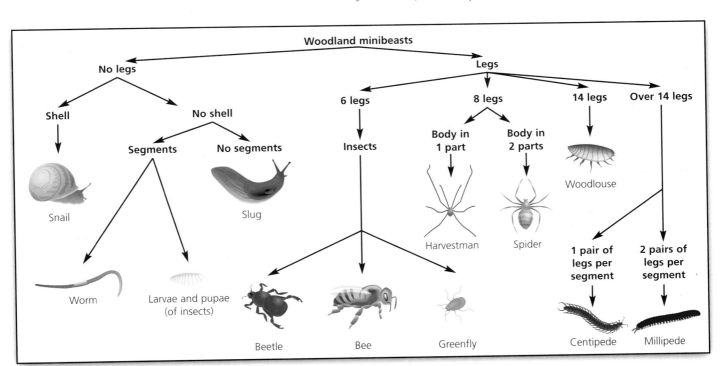

Grouping Organisms

Classifying Organisms

There are a huge variety of living organisms (e.g. animals and plants). Scientists **group** or **classify** them by their similarities and differences. This is important because it helps us to…

- work out how organisms evolved on Earth
- understand how organisms coexist in ecological communities
- identify and monitor rare organisms that are at risk from extinction.

Grouping Animals and Plants

Animals and **plants** can be identified quite easily because they have very different characteristics.

Members of the **animal kingdom**…

- move around
- are more compact (allows them to move around easily)
- cannot make their own food (they have to eat other living organisms).

Members of the **plant kingdom**…

- cannot move around
- have spreading roots and shoots (to enable them to get CO_2, minerals and water)
- have chloroplasts so they can make their own food (through photosynthesis).

Kingdoms
• Plants have cellulose cell walls. • Plants photosynthesise.
• Animals have a nervous system.

Vertebrates and Invertebrates

Animals can be divided into two sub-groups: some animals have backbones (**vertebrates**) and some do not (**invertebrates**).

The vertebrates can be classified further into groups with similar characteristics:

- **fish** have **wet scales** and **gills** which allow them to swim and breathe in water
- **amphibians** have a **moist permeable skin** which allows them to absorb oxygen from the water or from the air
- **reptiles** have **dry scales** preventing water loss on land
- **birds** have a **beak** and **feathers** which allow them to fly
- **mammals** have **fur** and **produce milk** to feed their young.

Vertebrates	Invertebrates
Fish	Annelids
Amphibians	Molluscs
Reptiles	Crustaceans
Birds	Arachnids
Mammals	Insects

Classification Difficulties

Some organisms are not easily classified.

Fungi (such as toadstools and mould) have to be grouped together in a separate kingdom because they do not fit the characteristics of either animals or of plants.

Fungi…
- cannot move around
- have spreading **hyphae** (fine threads) instead of roots
- cannot make their own food (they do not have chlorophyll so cannot carry out photosynthesis).

Euglena are microscopic green organisms which can photosynthesise but also move around. Are they plants or animals?

Archaeopteryx is an extinct organism identified from fossils. It seemed to have feathers like a bird, but no beak, and claws like a reptile. In which kingdom does it fit?

Species

Groups of organisms which share all the same characteristics are called **species**. Members of the same species are so similar that they can reproduce together.

A species is defined as 'a group of organisms which can freely interbreed to produce fertile offspring'. Each species is given two Latin names. This method of naming species is called the **binomial** ('two name') system.

Examples

Lions and tigers are very closely related species so they share the Latin **genus** name *panthera*. All lions belong to the same species so they have the species name *leo*. All tigers belong to the same species so they have the species name *tigris*.

New species are being identified all the time. Some ecosystems such as the ocean depths are relatively unexplored and potentially contain many undiscovered species.

Some organisms from different species can mate and reproduce to give birth to a **hybrid**. However, hybrids are not fertile, i.e. they cannot successfully reproduce themselves and so cannot be called a new species.

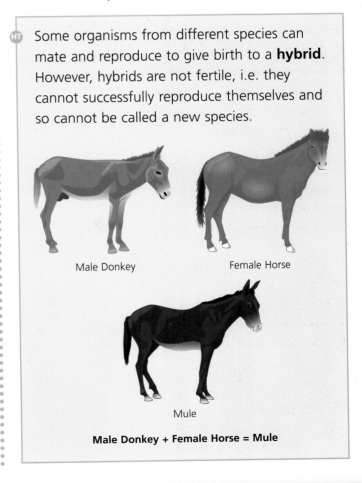

Male Donkey   Female Horse

Mule

Male Donkey + Female Horse = Mule

Grouping Organisms

Variation Within Species

Even within a species there can be a lot of variation. All dogs belong to the same species so they can reproduce between varieties to produce cross breeds.

Different Dog Breeds

Chihuahua   Papillon   Pug

Similar Species

Species which share a lot of common features tend to live in similar environments. They are adapted to compete for resources and survive under the same conditions.

However, very closely related species can be found living on different continents. Here the conditions may be different and so the species may have evolved over time to adapt to different conditions.

Species inherit their characteristics from their ancestors. We would expect similar species to be closely related through evolution to a **common ancestor**.

More About Similar Species

Organisms which have similar characteristics are not necessarily descended from a common ancestor. Sometimes they have just evolved to survive in the same environment and so have developed similar structures.

Whales, dolphins and sharks look quite similar: they have similar body shapes, flippers or fins and tails. However, they have descended from very **different evolutionary ancestors**. Their similarities are due to sharing a similar environment for thousands of years.

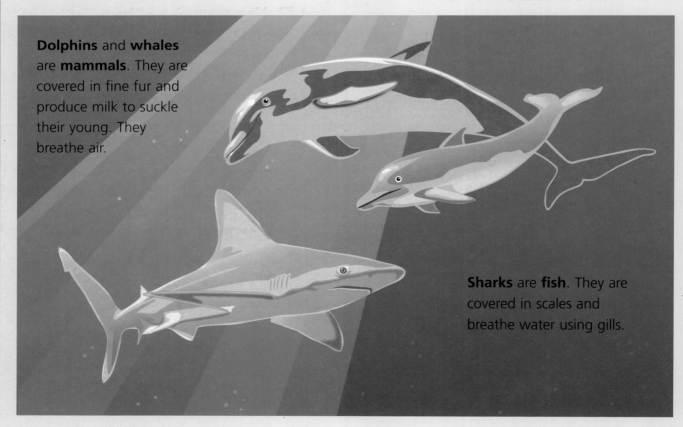

Dolphins and **whales** are **mammals**. They are covered in fine fur and produce milk to suckle their young. They breathe air.

Sharks are **fish**. They are covered in scales and breathe water using gills.

Making Food Using Energy from the Sun

Green plants do not absorb food from the soil. They make their own, using sunlight. This is called **photosynthesis** ('making through light') and it occurs in the cells. The diagram below shows what is needed and what is produced during photosynthesis.

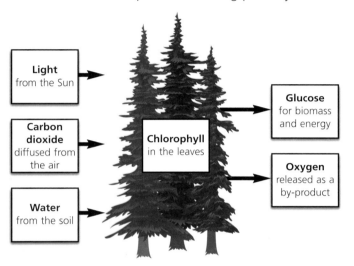

The word equation for photosynthesis is…

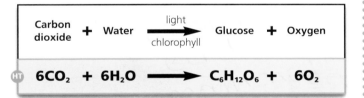

HT $$6CO_2 + 6H_2O \longrightarrow C_6H_{12}O_6 + 6O_2$$

Energy Use in Plants

The glucose produced in photosynthesis can be immediately used to produce energy through respiration. Some of this energy is used to build up smaller molecules into larger molecules.

Converting Glucose into Starch

The plant converts glucose into starch because starch is an insoluble carbohydrate, which can be stored in cells.

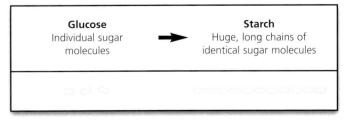

Converting Glucose into Cellulose

Cellulose is needed by the plant for cell walls. It is very similar to the structure of starch, but the long chains are cross-linked to form a meshwork. (You do not need to know the structure for your exam.)

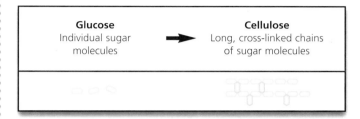

Converting Glucose, Nitrates and other Nutrients into Proteins

The plant needs protein for growth and repair and also to make enzymes.

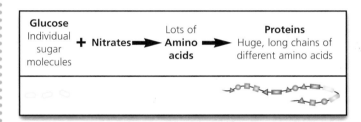

Converting Glucose into Lipids (Fats or Oils) to Store in Seeds

The glucose made in photosynthesis is *transported* as soluble sugars but is *stored* as insoluble starch.

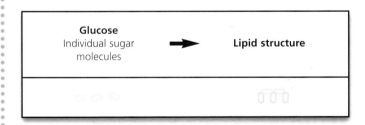

HT Starch is a very useful storage molecule. It is **insoluble** so it does not affect the concentration inside the cells where it is stored. If the cells stored soluble glucose, then the inside of the cells would become very concentrated and water would constantly move in, which would make the cell swell.

The Food Factory

Increasing Photosynthesis

Plants need light and warmth to grow. During winter, plant growth slows down, or even stops, due to the lack of sunlight and warmth. As spring arrives the plants start to grow again.

Plant growth, or the rate at which the plant photosynthesises, can be artificially increased by growing plants in greenhouses. This enables…
- the temperature to be increased by using heaters
- the light intensity to be increased by using lamps
- the carbon dioxide (CO_2) concentration to be increased by using chemicals (or as a by-product of the heaters).

Respiration in Plants

All living organisms (including plants) **respire** to supply their cells with the energy they need to work, grow and reproduce. Plants take in oxygen and use it to breakdown glucose to release energy:

Glucose + Oxygen ⟶ Carbon dioxide + Water + Energy

Rate of Photosynthesis

Temperature, **carbon dioxide concentration** and **light intensity** can interact to limit the **rate of photosynthesis**. At a particular time, any one of them may be the limiting factor.

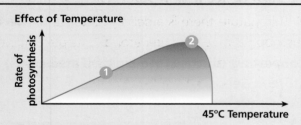

Effect of Temperature

Rate of photosynthesis / 45°C Temperature

1. As the temperature rises so does the rate of photosynthesis. This means temperature is limiting the rate of photosynthesis.
2. As the temperature approaches 45°C, the enzymes controlling photosynthesis start to be destroyed and the rate of photosynthesis declines to zero.

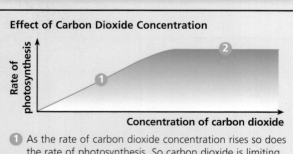

Effect of Carbon Dioxide Concentration

Rate of photosynthesis / Concentration of carbon dioxide

1. As the rate of carbon dioxide concentration rises so does the rate of photosynthesis. So carbon dioxide is limiting the rate of photosynthesis.
2. Rise in carbon dioxide levels now has no effect. Carbon dioxide is no longer the limiting factor; light or temperature must be.

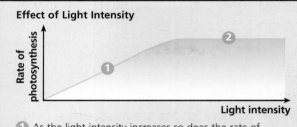

Effect of Light Intensity

Rate of photosynthesis / Light intensity

1. As the light intensity increases so does the rate of photosynthesis. This means light intensity is limiting the rate of photosynthesis.
2. Rise in light intensity now has no effect. Light intensity is no longer the limiting factor; carbon dioxide or temperature must be.

Respiration

During the day, light is available from the Sun so plants are able to photosynthesise; taking in carbon dioxide to make glucose and releasing oxygen as a by-product.

During the night, they respire, absorbing oxygen and giving out carbon dioxide. Respiration is the reverse of photosynthesis.

So, to summarise…

- during the day plants photosynthesise (absorb CO_2 and give out O_2)
- during the night plants respire (absorb O_2 and give out CO_2).

Factors Affecting Population Size

The size of any population of plants or animals will change over time. It can be affected by how well the populations compete for…

- food
- water
- shelter
- light
- minerals
- mates.

The better-adapted competitors will get most of the resources, so they can survive and produce offspring.

> **HT** Similar organisms living in the same habitat with the same prey and nesting sites occupy the same ecological niche.
>
> For example, red squirrels are the native species in the UK. When grey squirrels were introduced from the USA in 1876, both squirrel species had to compete for the same resources. Grey squirrels now outnumber red squirrels 66:1. Red squirrels are an **endangered species**.

Predators and Prey

Predators are animals that kill and eat other animals (e.g. foxes) while animals that are eaten are called the **prey** (e.g. rabbits).

Many animals can be both predator and prey, e.g. a stoat is a predator when it hunts rabbits and it is the prey when it is hunted by a fox.

Predator – Stoat   **Predator** – Fox

Prey – Rabbit   **Prey** – Stoat

Within nature there is a delicate balance between the population of the predator and its prey. However, the prey will always outnumber the predators.

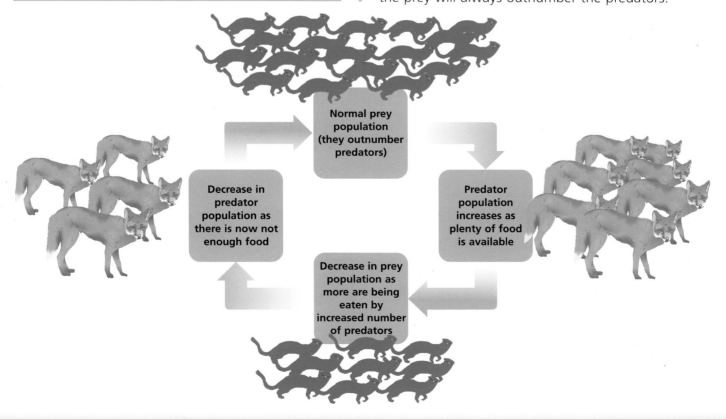

Normal prey population (they outnumber predators)

Predator population increases as plenty of food is available

Decrease in prey population as more are being eaten by increased number of predators

Decrease in predator population as there is now not enough food

Compete or Die

Interdependence of Organisms

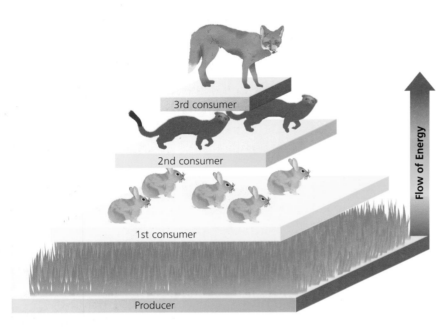

3rd consumer

2nd consumer

1st consumer

Producer

Flow of Energy

Opposite is an example of a food pyramid. An increase or decrease in the number of plants or animals at one stage in the food chain can affect the rest of the food chain. For example, if the rabbits in the pyramid were killed off by a disease…

- the number of stoats would decrease slightly because they have lost one of their food sources, this would then affect the foxes
- the stoats would have to find another source of food
- the number of lettuce and grass plants would increase as there are fewer rabbits eating them.

Parasitic Relationships

Parasites are groups of organisms that live off another living thing (known as the **host** organism). This can sometimes make the host organism ill or even kill it.

For example, humans (the host) can contract tapeworms (the parasite) by eating pork infected with tapeworm larvae (also known as bladderworms). Once inside a person's body, the larvae attach themselves to the wall of the gut, and a young tapeworm grows. The tapeworm then absorbs food from the person's gut.

Mutualistic Relationships

In mutualistic relationships, two organisms form a relationship from which both organisms benefit.

For example, oxpecker birds get a ready supply of food from the ticks and flies on a buffalo's skin. And the buffalo also benefits as the birds get rid of the pests and provide an early warning system by hissing when lions or other predators approach.

Predator–Prey Cycles

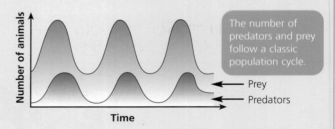

Number of animals

Time

The number of predators and prey follow a classic population cycle.

Prey

Predators

Using the food pyramid above as an example, there will always be more stoats than foxes and the population peak for the fox will always come after the population peak for the stoat.

Mutualistic Relationships

The interdependence of organisms dictates where they will be found and in what numbers. Leguminous plants, e.g. the pea plant, have root nodules that contain nitrogen-fixing bacteria, which take sugars from the plant to use in respiration and convert nitrogen into nitrates that the plant can absorb. Leguminous plants are able to survive in nitrogen-poor soils because of their mutualistic relationship with the bacteria.

Adaptations

Adaptations are special features or behaviour which make an organism especially well suited to its environment, and better able to compete with other organisms for limited resources.

An adaptation can be thought of as a **biological solution** to an environmental challenge. Evolution provides the solution and makes species fit their environment.

Life in a Very Hot Climate – The Camel

- Large surface area to volume ratio to increase heat loss.
- Body fat stored in hump so very little insulating layer beneath the skin.
- Loses very little water in sweat or urine.
- Able to tolerate changes in body temperature so does not need to sweat so much.
- Large feet to spread its weight on the sand.
- Bushy eyelashes and hair-lined nostrils stop sand from entering.

Life in a Very Cold Climate – The Polar Bear

- Small ears and large bulk both reduce the surface area to volume ratio to reduce heat loss.
- Large amount of insulating fat (blubber) beneath the skin.
- Thick white fur for insulation and camouflage.
- Large feet to spread its weight on snow and ice.
- Fur on the soles of its paws gives insulation and grip.
- Powerful legs so it is a good swimmer which enables it to catch its food.
- Sharp claws and teeth to capture prey.

As plants and animals become better adapted to their environment their population size and distribution can increase.

A camel

A polar bear

Plant Adaptations

Plants also adapt to enable them to survive in a competitive environment.

Life in a Very Hot Climate – The Cactus

- Rounded shape reduces water loss by giving a small surface area to volume ratio.
- Thick waxy cuticle to reduce water loss.
- Stores water in spongy layer inside its stem to resist drought.
- Leaves reduced to spines to reduce water loss and protect the cacti from predators.
- Green stem so that the plant can photosynthesise without leaves.
- Long roots to reach water.

Pollinating Flowers

Flowers have several methods of spreading pollen:

- **by wind** – pollen is small and light so it is easily carried on the wind. Pollen is collected by large, feathery stigma which hang outside the flower
- **by insects** – colourful petals attract the insect into the flower to reach the nectar (its food). The sticky pollen gets trapped on the insect's hairs, and is rubbed off onto the next plant it visits.

Effect of Adaptations

Tigers are native to certain parts of Northern India and are adapted to life in the semi-jungle areas of that region. However, the range (distribution) of the tiger has been increased by subtle adaptations which have enabled them to spread into more regions. For example, the tigers of Siberia are much paler in colour and have longer, thicker fur than those of Northern India. Those tigers who moved northwards were 'shaped' by evolutionary forces so that they were well adapted to their environment.

Adapt to Fit

Animal Adaptations

Animals have developed in many different ways to become well adapted to their environment to help them to survive. Some examples are given below.

Earthworms eat their way through the soil. To help them do this they secrete mucus to lubricate their passage. They also have tiny bristles to help them grip the sides of the burrow.

To enable them to fly, birds have feathered wings with a large surface area to create the thrust needed for flight and they have very light bones with a honeycomb structure to reduce weight. Their aerodynamic shape reduces air resistance.

Fish have a very streamlined shape to reduce resistance as they swim through the water. Their scale-covered skin is smooth to reduce friction. They have different fins to propel them, to change direction and to prevent rolling during swimming. Fish use gills to allow them to breathe in water.

Plant Adaptations

Plants have also adapted to suit their environment. For example...

- cacti have a thick, waxy cuticle and leaves reduced to spines to limit water loss. Their long roots reach underground water, which they store in the fleshy stem
- the rubber plant has thick waxy leaves and produces many roots to find water in its hot, tropical environment.

Eat or Be Eaten

Carnivores eat other animals, so they must be successfully adapted to be good predators.

For example, lions are excellent predators. They are built for bursts of speed but camouflaged to avoid being spotted until the last moment. They have sharp teeth and claws to grab and kill their prey. The lion's eyes are positioned at the front of their head, providing three-dimensional vision and accurate perception of size and distance.

Herbivores eat plants and are prey for predators like lions. They too must be well adapted to escape.

For example, gazelles are well-camouflaged in their environment and live in groups, increasing the opportunities for detecting and confusing predators. Their eyes are positioned on the side of their head for 360° vision so that they can see predators approaching whilst grazing. Also, they are built for speed so they can escape quickly.

Some prey use defence mechanisms such as stings or poisons to defend themselves against attack.

Survival of the Fittest

The Fossil Record

Fossils are the remains of plants or animals from thousands of years ago which have been preserved in sedimentary rock. Fossilisation usually occurs in the hard parts of organisms (such as shells, bones, leaves) which do not decay easily, or when the soft parts of organisms are replaced by minerals as they decay.

The fossilised animal or plant remains leave a cast or imprint in the rock which forms around them. Sometimes whole specimens can be preserved intact in peat bogs, ice, tar pits or amber when the conditions for decay are absent, e.g. oxygen, moisture, temperature or correct pH.

Animals and plants gradually change (**evolve**) over a long period of time. The fossilised remains show a record of these changes.

Evolution of Ammonites

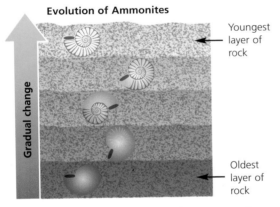

Youngest layer of rock

Gradual change

Oldest layer of rock

Although the fossil record lets us see how organisms have changed, it is incomplete because…

- some body parts, particularly soft tissue, may not have been fossilised
- fossilisation occurs only rarely since the conditions have to be just right
- rock geology may have changed, so some fossils may have been lost
- many, many fossils are still out there to be discovered.

> **HT** The fossil record led to a furious debate about how they got there, particularly during the 19th century. Some notable religious figures suggested that the fossil record had been created by God.

The Theory Of Evolution

The Theory of Evolution states that all living things which exist today, and many more that are now extinct, have evolved from simple life forms, which first developed 3 000 000 000 (3 billion) years ago.

Evolution is the slow, continual change of organisms over a very long period to become better **adapted to their environment**. These adaptations are controlled by genes and can be passed on to future generations.

If the **environment changes**, species must change with it if they are to survive. Some animal and plant species will **evolve** and **survive**, by a process called **natural selection** (see p.68). Species which are not well-adapted to their environment may become **extinct**.

The Evolution of Horses

By looking at fossils we can see that the first horses were small, almost dog-like creatures which lived in the forests of North America around 55 million years ago. They had toes on their feet to enable them to move around the forest floor and small teeth adapted to a diet of fruit and leaves.

The fossil record shows that the horses gradually changed at around the same time as the forests dried out and became grasslands. They evolved to become larger in size; their toes fused together to form a hoof, which would be ideal for running on hard ground; and their teeth became large, which enabled them to grind tough grass.

This is an example of how species can change to adapt to their environment.

Survival of the Fittest

Examples of Natural Selection

Peppered Moths

Most **peppered moths** are pale and speckled. They are easily **camouflaged** amongst the lichen on silver birch tree bark. There are some rare, darker coloured varieties of the peppered moth, but they are easily seen and eaten by birds.

However, in areas with high levels of air pollution, lichens die and the bark becomes discoloured with soot. The darker coloured moths are now at an advantage, they survive and breed in greater numbers, whilst the pale moths are eaten by birds.

Penicillin-resistant Bacteria

The resistance of some bacteria to penicillin is an increasing problem and is caused by a mutation in the bacteria. The bacteria became resistant to penicillin by natural selection, as follows:

1. **variation** – bacteria mutated. Some were resistant to the antibiotic penicillin, others were not
2. **competition** – the non-resistant bacteria were more likely to be killed by the penicillin
3. **best adapted** – the penicillin-resistant bacteria survived and reproduced more often
4. **pass on their genes** – more bacteria are becoming resistant to penicillin. This is a major health issue.

This is why doctors are reluctant to prescribe antibiotics unless they are absolutely necessary.

Warfarin-resistant Rats

Rats are a pest in urban and rural environments. One way of dealing with rats is to put out poisoned food to kill them. An effective poison is warfarin, which prevents blood clotting so the rats slowly bleed to death. Warfarin has been so widely used that a breed of 'super-rats' has emerged. Mutant rats able to resist warfarin are not killed by the poison and so survive with less competition for food from other rats. They breed and pass on their warfarin-resistant genes. Now there are large populations of rats which cannot be controlled using warfarin.

Peppered Moths

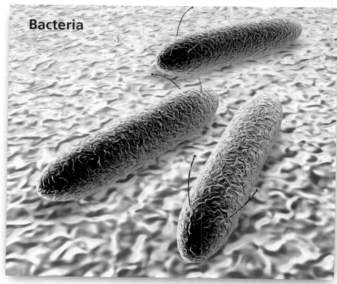

Bacteria

New Species Emerge

Species become more and more specialised as they evolve, adapting to their environmental conditions.

Groups of the same species who are separated from each other by physical boundaries like mountains or sea will not be able to breed and share their genes.

Over long periods of time, the separate groups may specialise so much that they cannot successfully breed any longer and so two new species have formed.

Jean-Baptiste Lamarck

Before Darwin developed his theory, Lamarck suggested that evolution happened by the inheritance of acquired characteristics:

- organisms change during their lifetime as they struggle to survive
- these changes are passed on to their offspring.

For example, he suggested that when giraffes stretch their necks to reach leaves higher on the trees, this extra neck length can be passed on to their offspring.

Lamarck's theory was rejected because there was no evidence that the changes that happened in an individual's lifetime could alter their genes and so be passed on to their offspring.

Charles Darwin

Darwin made four very important observations.

1. All living things produce far more offspring than actually survive to adulthood.
2. In spite of this, population sizes remain fairly constant, due to predation, etc.
3. There is variation in members of the same species.
4. Characteristics can be passed on from one generation to the next.

From these observations Darwin deduced that all organisms were involved in a struggle for survival in which only the best adapted organisms would survive, reproduce and pass on their characteristics. This formed the basis for his famous theory of **Evolution by Natural Selection**.

The reaction to Darwin's theory, particularly from religious authorities, was hostile since they felt he was saying that 'men were descended from monkeys' (although he was not) and that he was denying God's role in the creation of man. This meant that his theory was only slowly and reluctantly accepted by many people in spite of the great number of eminent supporters he had.

Evolution by Natural Selection

Evolution is the change in a population over a large number of generations that may result in the formation of a new species, the members of which are better adapted to their environment.

There are four key points to remember.

1. Individuals within a population show **variation** (i.e. differences due to their genes).
2. There is **competition** between individuals for food, mates, etc. and also predation and disease, which keep population sizes constant in spite of the production of many offspring, i.e. there is a 'struggle for survival', and many individuals die.
3. Individuals which are better **adapted** to the environment are more likely to survive, breed successfully and produce offspring. This is termed 'survival of the fittest'.
4. These **survivors** will therefore pass on their genes to these offspring resulting in an improved organism being evolved through natural selection.

Species which are unable to compete become **extinct**.

Population Out of Control?

The Population Explosion

The human population is increasing exponentially (at a rapidly increasing rate). This is creating three major issues...

1. the use of finite resources like fossil fuels and minerals is increasing
2. the production of pollution, in particular household waste, sewage, sulfur dioxide and carbon dioxide, is increasing.
3. ever-increasing competition for basic resources, i.e. food and water.

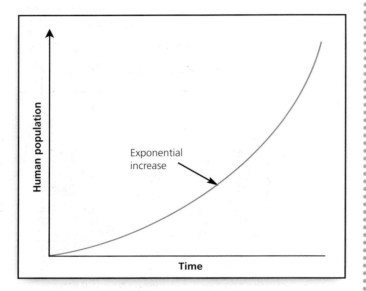

Ozone Depletion

Ozone is a natural gas found high up in the Earth's atmosphere which prevents too many harmful ultraviolet (UV) rays reaching the Earth.

Recently, scientists have noticed that the ozone layer is becoming thinner and more people are suffering from skin cancer. This is because the thinner ozone is unable to block out as much of the UV rays.

Many people blame the use of CFCs (chlorofluorocarbons) in factories, fridges and aerosol cans for this change in the ozone layer.

Acid Rain

When coal or oils are burnt, sulfur dioxide is produced. Sulfur dioxide gas dissolves in water to produce acid rain (see diagram below). Acid rain can...
- damage trees, stonework and metals
- make rivers and lakes acidic which means some organisms can no longer survive.

The acids can be carried a long way away from the factories where they are produced. Acid rain falling in one country could be the result of fossil fuels being burned in another country.

> **HT** Although the developed countries of the world (e.g. USA, UK, France and Japan) have a small proportion of the world's population, they have the greatest impact on the use of resources and production of pollution.
>
> Many countries are now trying to agree limits on the production of pollution, increase trade and cancel the debts of the world's poorest countries.

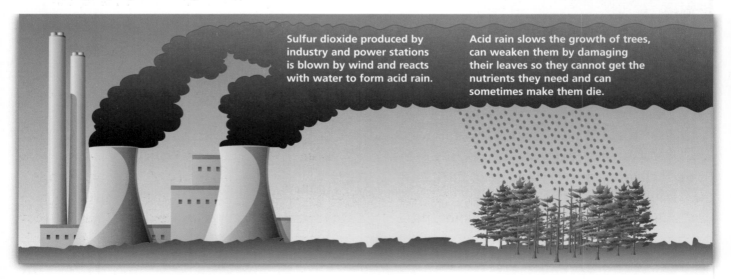

Sulfur dioxide produced by industry and power stations is blown by wind and reacts with water to form acid rain.

Acid rain slows the growth of trees, can weaken them by damaging their leaves so they cannot get the nutrients they need and can sometimes make them die.

The Greenhouse Effect and Global Warming

Heat energy from the Sun reaches Earth in the form of radiation. Some of this energy is reflected back out towards space. When it reaches the atmosphere some rays pass through, but others are trapped in. It is these trapped rays that keep the Earth warmer than it would be otherwise. This is known as the **greenhouse effect**.

However, because the amount of carbon dioxide in the atmosphere has now increased, this has led to more of the energy being reflected back. This is known as **global warming** because the Earth is gradually getting hotter. Only a few degrees Celsius rise in temperature may lead to climate changes and a rise in sea levels.

Global Warming

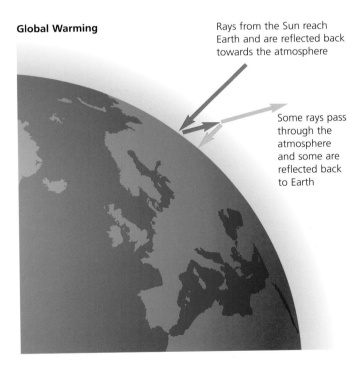

Rays from the Sun reach Earth and are reflected back towards the atmosphere

Some rays pass through the atmosphere and some are reflected back to Earth

Living Organisms as Indicators

Pollution is one of the environmental factors that can drastically affect the survival of living organisms. Some organisms are very sensitive to pollution, so they die. Other species have evolved to resist the toxic effects of pollution and so can survive. These are called **indicator species**. Two examples of indicator species are lichens and insect larvae.

Lichens

Different types of lichens have differing levels of sensitivity to sulfur dioxide pollution in the air. The more resilient varieties are able to survive even when high levels of sulfur dioxide are found in the air. The more sensitive ones cannot, which causes them to die.

The distribution of lichens acts as a good indicator of the concentration of sulfur dioxide in the air. For example, if you look at the lichens found on trees close to a busy road, you will find a few varieties of lichen. However, as you get further away from the road, you will notice that you will find more, and a wider variety of, lichens on the trees. This is because the sulfur dioxide is less intense further away from the road, so more varieties are able to flourish.

Few varieties of lichens indicate high concentration of sulfur dioxide in the air

Many varieties of lichens indicate low concentration of sulfur dioxide in the air

Insect Larvae

Insect larvae can act as an indicator of water pollution. When sewage works outflow into streams, this pollutes the water by altering the levels of nitrogen compounds in the stream. This then has an impact on the organisms that can survive in the stream.

Organisms that can cope with high levels of nitrogen include the rat-tailed maggot, the blood worm, the waterlouse and the sludgeworm. These species are all tolerant of water pollution. However, some organisms are very sensitive to this type of water pollution so they are not found in areas where there is a high concentration of nitrogen compounds. Organisms such as mayfly and stonefly larvae are killed by high levels of water pollution so they are indicators of clean water.

Sustainability

Sustainable Development

As the world's population grows there is an increasing demand for food and energy, and more waste products are created.

Sustainable development is concerned with ensuring that resources can be maintained in the long-term at a level that allows appropriate consumption or use by people. This often requires limiting exploitation by using quotas or ensuring the resources are replenished or restocked.

Cod in the North Sea

The UK has one of the largest sea fishing industries in Europe. To ensure the industry can continue and cod stocks can be conserved, quotas are set to prevent over-fishing.

In 2006 the European Union Fisheries Council made changes which included…

- increasing mesh size to prevent young cod being caught before they reach breeding age
- increasing quotas of certain types of fish other than cod.

Pine Forests in Scandinavia

Scandinavia uses a lot of pine wood to make furniture, paper and provide energy. To ensure the long-term economic viability of pine-related industries, companies replenish and restock the pine forests by planting a new sapling for each mature tree they cut down.

Endangered Species

Endangered species are those that are in danger of becoming extinct unless something is done to prevent it. The survival of plant or animal species can be threatened for a number of reasons…

- climate change
- new predators – hunted by humans and by animals introduced by humans
- habitat destruction, e.g. by logging companies – wipes out food source and shelter
- hunting – reduces the population size
- competition – has to compete for food, shelter, etc.
- pollution – marine mammals accumulate toxic pollutants from their food.

The habitats of endangered species should be conserved. When countries or companies neglect this idea various species can become endangered, for example…

- the **red kite** was exploited for its feathers
- the **osprey's** habitats were destroyed
- the **red squirrel** had to compete with the grey squirrel when it was introduced to England.

Education is a powerful 'weapon' in promoting the ideas behind sustainable development, and many endangered species are now protected:

- The Countryside Council for Wales provides legal protection for red squirrels. They cannot be trapped, killed or kept, except under special licence.
- The red kite and osprey both have protected sites in Wales where they can live and breed undisturbed.

There are endangered species all over the world. For example, in China, the panda is endangered because it is so well-adapted to its environment it cannot survive anywhere else. And the gorilla became endangered as a result of deforestation.

If endangered species are not protected they could become extinct like the mammoth, the dodo and the sabre-toothed tiger.

Protecting Endangered Species

Endangered species can be protected from extinction:

- education can help to protect endangered species by promoting sustainable development
- animals can be bred in captivity (e.g. zoos) and possibly returned to their natural habitat to create new populations
- protecting the natural habitat (for example, by creating Sites of Special Scientific Interest) or creating artificial ecosystems (e.g. zoos, aquariums) provide good conditions for the species to live in
- hunting legally protected species can be prohibited.

Whales

There are many different whale species, but some of these are now endangered; they are close to extinction. The main causes of whale deaths are:

- getting entangled in fishing nets and drowning
- being affected by pollutants in the sea – whales are at the top of the food chain, so they accumulate pollutants from their food
- colliding with ships during migration
- effects of climate change affecting food source
- culling and hunting – to reduce the population size to prevent competition with the fishing industry
- hunting – to provide food.

Money can be made from whales whether they are dead or alive. Live whales can be a big tourist attraction, but dead whales can be used for food, oil and to make cosmetics. Conservation campaigns have made people much more aware of the plight of whales. One method of conserving whales has been to keep them in captivity. Some zoos have had success with captive breeding. It enables whale behaviour to be studied so we can understand them and protect them more efficiently.

However, a captive whale suffers a huge loss of freedom being reared in a zoo rather than in its natural habitat. People argue that captive whales do not behave naturally. Many captive whales are tamed and trained to perform for the public.

Conservation Programmes

Sustainability requires planning and co-operation at local, national and international levels. Conservation programmes have an essential role in…

- protecting the human food supply by maintaining the genetic variety of crop animals and plants
- stabilising ecosystems by ensuring minimal damage to food chains and habitats
- studying and identifying plants which might be useful to develop medicines to treat diseases
- protecting the culture of indigenous people living in threatened habitats such as the Amazonian rainforest.

Conservation is difficult. For example, we need to know much more about whales to protect them effectively. At the moment, our knowledge of how whales communicate over large distances, how they migrate and how they dive and survive at extreme depths (remember whales are air-breathing mammals) is quite limited. Studying whales in captivity can be misleading but is easier than trying to study whales free in the ocean!

Different countries take very different points of view on issues like whaling. The International Whaling Commission makes laws to protect whale species and sets quotas for hunting. It is very difficult to enforce these laws though because it is impossible to police all the world's oceans. It is also difficult to get all countries to agree. Many countries support the idea that whale hunting is unnecessary. However, some countries like Iceland, Norway and Japan disagree with a ban on killing whales. They feel it is necessary to preserve the fishing industry and carry out 'research culls' to investigate the effect of whale population size on fish stocks.

Fundamental Chemical Concepts

For this unit you need to know all the chemical concepts that were introduced in Chemistry Unit C1.

Make sure you remember…

- the names of the parts of an atom – the atomic particles – and their relative charges
- the difference between an element, a compound and a mixture
- the difference between ionic and covalent bonds
- how to use the periodic table
- the chemical symbols for the most common elements
- the chemical formulae for the most common compounds
- how to write displayed formula (including how to represent double carbon carbon bonds)
- how to write a word equation for a chemical reaction (including labelling the reactants and the products)
- how to balance a symbol equation (see below).

If you are unfamiliar with any of the terms above, refer back to Fundamental Chemical Concepts in Unit 1 (see p.24–26) to refresh your memory.

HT You need to know the formulae for the following compounds:

- **calcium carbonate, $CaCO_3$**
- **calcium chloride, $CaCl_2$**
- **carbon dioxide, CO_2**
- **carbon monoxide, CO**
- **ethane, C_2H_6**
- **hydrochloric acid, HCl**
- **hydrogen, H_2**
- **magnesium chloride, $MgCl_2$**
- **methane, CH_4**
- **oxygen, O_2**
- **water, H_2O.**

Try to learn as many of the formulae in this book as you can – it will help you in your exams.

Balancing Equations

	Reactants		⟶	Products		
① Write a word equation	Sodium	+ Water	⟶	Sodium hydroxide	+	Hydrogen
② Substitute in formulae	**Na**	+ H_2O	⟶	**NaOH**	+	H_2

③ Balance the equation

- First we need to add another **NaOH** to the product side and a H_2O to the reactant side to balance the **H**s and the **O**s.
- Then we need to add another **Na** to the reactant side to balance the **Na**s.
- There are now 2 **Na**s, 4 **H**s and 2 **O**s on each side – **it is balanced!**

④ Write a balanced symbol equation

2Na	+	**2H₂O**	⟶	**2NaOH**	+	**H₂**

$$2Na + 2H_2O \longrightarrow 2NaOH + H_2$$

Paint

Paint is a mixture of different materials. It is a special mixture called a **colloid**. In a colloid, fine solid particles are well mixed with liquid particles but they are not dissolved.

Paint is a mixture of…
- a **pigment**, a finely powdered solid that has a strong colour – it forms a colloid with the binding medium
- a **binding medium** – an oil that sticks the pigment to the surface it is being painted onto
- a **solvent** – dissolves the thick binding medium and makes it easier to coat the surface.

The paint coats a surface with a thin layer and the solvent evaporates away as the paint dries. The solvent in **emulsion** paint is **water**. In **oil-based** paints, the pigment is dispersed in an **oil** (the binding medium). Often, there is a solvent present that dissolves the oil.

Paint can be used to protect or to decorate a surface.

Dyes

Dyes are substances used to colour fabrics. Some dyes are made from natural sources such as onion skins or cochineal (a red-coloured insect), but most are manufactured (**synthetic**). Synthetic dyes tend to be more vivid and are able to produce a much greater range of colours.

Special Pigments

Thermochromic pigments change colour when they are heated or cooled. These pigments can be used to coat kettles and cups to indicate that they are hot.

Phosphorescent pigments glow in the dark. They absorb and store energy and release it as light when it is dark. The paint on some watch dials contains phosphorescent pigments.

More about Paint

The particle size of the solids in a colloid must be very small so they stay scattered throughout the mixture. If the particles are too big, they would start to settle down to the bottom.

An oil-based paint such as a gloss paint dries in two stages:
1 The solvent **evaporates** away.
2 The oil-binding medium reacts with oxygen in the air as it dries to form a hard layer. This is an **oxidation** reaction.

More about Pigments

There are only a few thermochromic pigments. To increase the range of colours they can be mixed with ordinary pigments, e.g.

Ordinary pigment + Thermochromic pigment = Mixture colour

Thermochromic pigments change to colourless as it gets hotter and so the paint changes from the mixture colour to the ordinary pigment colour.

Cold   Hot

The first 'glow in the dark' paints were made using radioactive materials as pigments. They were used to paint the dials on aircraft instrument panels and the first luminous watches. However, the people who painted with these pigments were exposed to too much radiation and some of them developed cancer as a result. Phosphorescent pigments are not radioactive, so they are much safer to use.

Construction Materials

Materials

The following materials are used in the construction industry (particularly in the construction of buildings):

- aluminium
- iron
- brick
- cement
- concrete
- glass
- granite
- limestone
- marble.

Materials from Rocks

Many construction materials come from rocks found in the Earth's crust.

- The metals **iron** and **aluminium** have to be extracted from rocks called ores.
- Clay is a rock that makes **brick** when it is baked.
- Glass is made from sand, which is small grains of rock.

Some rocks, like limestone, marble and granite, just need to be shaped to be ready to use as a building material. Limestone is the easiest to shape because it is the softest; marble is harder to shape and granite is harder still.

Rock is dug out of the ground in mines and quarries. Mining and quarrying companies have to take steps to reduce their impact on the local area and environment because mines and quarries can…

- be noisy
- be dusty
- take up land
- change the shape of the landscape
- increase the local road traffic.

A responsible company will also ensure it reconstructs, covers up and restores any area it has worked on.

Limestone and marble are both forms of calcium carbonate ($CaCO_3$). When calcium carbonate is heated it breaks up into calcium oxide and carbon dioxide.

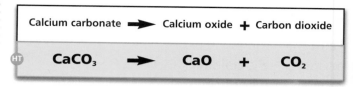

Calcium carbonate $\longrightarrow$ Calcium oxide $+$ Carbon dioxide

HT $CaCO_3 \longrightarrow CaO + CO_2$

This type of reaction is called a **thermal decomposition**; one material breaks down into two new substances when it is heated.

When clay and limestone are heated together, **cement** is made. One of the main uses of cement is to make **concrete**.

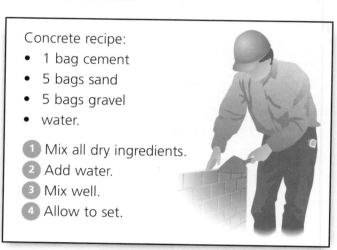

Concrete recipe:
- 1 bag cement
- 5 bags sand
- 5 bags gravel
- water.

1. Mix all dry ingredients.
2. Add water.
3. Mix well.
4. Allow to set.

Concrete is very hard but not very strong. It can be strengthened by allowing it to set around steel rods to reinforce it. **Reinforced concrete** is a **composite material**.

HT More about Materials

Rocks differ in hardness because of the ways in which they were made. Limestone is a **sedimentary** rock. Marble is a **metamorphic** rock made from limestone that has been put under pressure and heated, which makes it harder. The hardest rock, granite, is an **igneous** rock.

A composite material combines the best properties of each material. Reinforced concrete combines the strength and flexibility of the steel bars with the hardness of the concrete. Reinforced concrete has many more uses than ordinary concrete.

Does the Earth Move?

Structure of the Earth

The Earth is nearly spherical and has a layered structure as shown below.

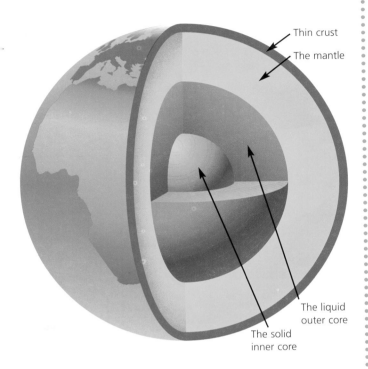

Thin crust
The mantle
The liquid outer core
The solid inner core

The thickness of the thin, rocky **crust** varies between 10km and 100km. **Oceanic** crust lies beneath the oceans. **Continental** crust forms the continents.

The **mantle** extends almost halfway to the centre of the Earth. It has a higher density than rock in the crust, and has a different composition.

> **HT** Just below the crust, the mantle is relatively cold and rigid. However, at greater depths it becomes hot and non-rigid which means it can flow.

The **core** accounts for over half of the Earth's radius. It is made of nickel and iron and has a liquid outer part and a solid inner part.

It is difficult to collect information about the structure of the Earth. The deepest mines and deepest holes drilled into the crust have penetrated only a few kilometres. Scientists have to rely on studying the seismic waves (vibrations) caused by earthquakes.

Movement of the Lithosphere

The Earth's **lithosphere** is the relatively cold, rigid, outer part of the Earth, consisting of the crust and outer part of the mantle. The top of the lithosphere is 'cracked' into several large interlocking pieces called **tectonic plates** (see below).

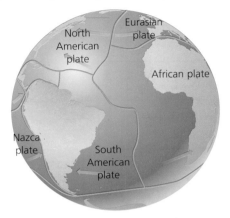

The plates sit on top of the mantle because they are less dense than the mantle itself. Although there does not appear to be much going on, the Earth and its crust are very dynamic. They move slowly, at speeds of a few centimetres a year. Plates can move apart, towards each other, or slide past each other. This movement causes **earthquakes** and **volcanoes** at the boundaries between plates.

Volcanoes

Volcanoes form where molten rock can find its way through to the Earth's surface, usually at plate boundaries or where the crust is very thin.

Living near a volcano can be very dangerous, but people often choose to live there because volcanic soil is very fertile.

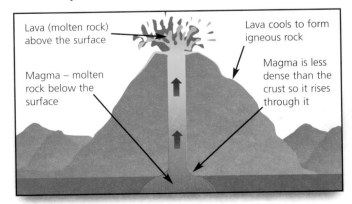

Lava (molten rock) above the surface
Lava cools to form igneous rock
Magma – molten rock below the surface
Magma is less dense than the crust so it rises through it

Does the Earth Move?

Forming Rock

Igneous rock is formed from molten **magma** which has either come up to the surface or has been trapped beneath it. These rocks are very hard and consist of interlocking crystals which are large if the rock has cooled slowly, and small if it has cooled quickly. The table below shows how four types of igneous rock are formed:

Cooling	Iron-rich lava	Silica-rich lava
Fast-cooling rock forms small crystals.	Basalt	Rhyolite
Slow-cooling rock forms large crystals.	Gabbro	Granite

Basalt

Rhyolite

Gabbro

Granite

ⱨⱦ Magma

The different compositions of magma affect the type of rock that will form, and the type of eruption.

Iron-rich basalt magma is quite runny in comparison to silica-rich rhyolite, which is thicker, and treacle-like. Rhyolite magma produces pumice, volcanic ash and bombs. The volcanoes that have thicker magma can erupt violently with disastrous effects.

Geologists study volcanoes to help understand the structure of the Earth and also to help predict when eruptions will occur to give an early warning for people who live nearby. However, they still cannot predict with 100% certainty.

What Causes Plates to Move?

Just below the crust, the mantle is relatively cold and rigid. At greater depths the mantle is hot, non-rigid and able to flow. Within the mantle, at these greater depths, are convection currents (see p.79) which are driven by heat

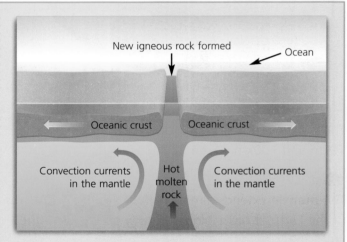

New igneous rock formed

Ocean

Oceanic crust

Oceanic crust

Convection currents in the mantle

Hot molten rock

Convection currents in the mantle

released from radioactivity. These convection currents cause molten rock (magma) to rise to the surface at the boundaries. The hot molten rock then solidifies to form new igneous rock. This slow movement of the magma causes the **plates to move apart** (as indicated by the arrows).

As more magma escapes through the 'fracture', huge mountain ranges are created under the oceans. These mountains are symmetrically arranged on either side of the boundary giving rise to mid-oceanic ridges and **rift valleys** under the oceans.

Effects of Plate Collision

Whilst some plates around the world are moving **apart**, others are moving **towards** each other. Because oceanic crust has a higher density than continental crust, an oceanic plate 'dips down' when it collides with a continental plate and slides under it. This is called **subduction**.

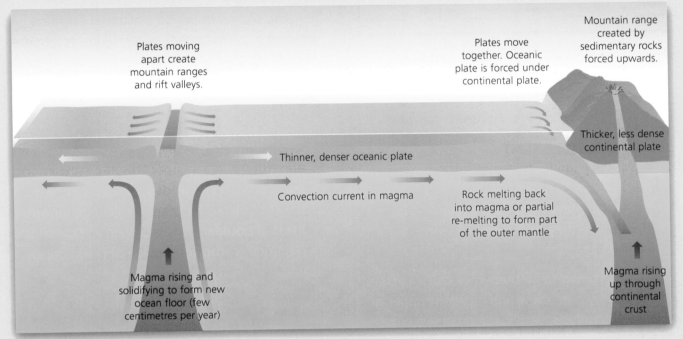

Plates moving apart create mountain ranges and rift valleys.

Plates move together. Oceanic plate is forced under continental plate.

Mountain range created by sedimentary rocks forced upwards.

Thicker, less dense continental plate

Thinner, denser oceanic plate

Convection current in magma

Rock melting back into magma or partial re-melting to form part of the outer mantle

Magma rising and solidifying to form new ocean floor (few centimetres per year)

Magma rising up through continental crust

Developing a Theory

Scientists noticed that...

- the continents seemed to fit together like a jigsaw
- the geology of Scotland and Canada was similar, as was the geology of Africa and South America
- similar animal species were found on either side of the Atlantic, e.g. caribou in Canada and reindeer in Scandinavia.

They developed the idea that millions of years ago all the continents were joined together. Studying the formation of new rock at oceanic plate boundaries shows that the plates are moving apart. The age of rock increases as you move away from the boundary.

How it once was

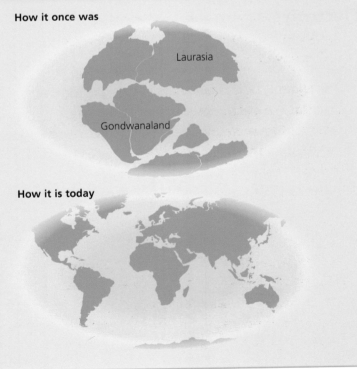

Laurasia

Gondwanaland

How it is today

Metals and Alloys

Copper

Copper is a very useful metal because it is an excellent conductor of heat and it does not corrode. Copper is made by heating naturally-occurring copper ore with carbon. The ore breaks down to copper oxide and the carbon then removes the oxygen, leaving the copper.

$$\text{Copper oxide} + \text{Carbon} \longrightarrow \text{Copper} + \text{Carbon dioxide}$$

The process uses lots of energy, which makes it expensive. It is cheaper to recycle copper than to extract it from its ore. Recycling also conserves our limited supply of copper ore. However, there are some problems with recycling copper.

Recycling copper can be more difficult if it has other metals stuck to it or mixed with it. If the copper is very impure, it would then have to be purified using electrolysis (see below) before it could be used again.

Copper that is going to be used in electrical circuits needs to be very pure. New and recycled copper is purified by **electrolysis**, which is an expensive process.

Electrolysis

Electrolysis is the breaking down of a compound made up of ions into simpler substances using an electric current. During electrolysis, ions gain or lose electrons at the electrodes, forming electrically neutral atoms or molecules which are then released.

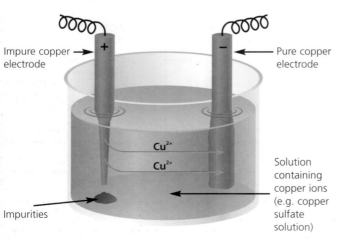

Impure copper electrode

Pure copper electrode

Cu^{2+}

Cu^{2+}

Solution containing copper ions (e.g. copper sulfate solution)

Impurities

To electrolyse copper, a negative electrode made of pure copper and a positive electrode made of impure copper are inserted into a solution that contains copper ions, such as copper sulfate solution.

An electric current is then passed through the solution. The pure copper moves from the positive electrode to the negative electrode and the impurities fall to the bottom of the solution.

The pure copper (negative electrode) can then be removed to be made into wires, pipes, etc. Some valuable metals can be extracted from the impurities.

> **HT** **Electrolysis** is the name given to a chemical reaction that uses electricity. The electricity is passed through a liquid or a solution called an **electrolyte**, e.g. copper (II) sulfate is used to purify copper. **Electrodes** are used to connect to the electrolyte. The positive electrode (**anode**) is made of **boulder** (impure copper) and the negative electrode (**cathode**) is made of pure copper.

Alloys

An alloy is a mixture of a metal with another element (usually another metal). Alloys, e.g. bronze and steel, are made to improve the properties of a metal and to make them more useful – they are often harder and stronger than the pure metal.

- **Amalgam** is made using mercury and is used for fillings in teeth.
- **Brass** (made of copper and zinc) is used in door handles and ornaments.
- **Solder** (made of lead and tin) is used to join pipes and wires.

> **HT** ## Smart Alloys
>
> A **smart alloy** such as **nitinol** (an alloy of nickel and titanium) can be bent and twisted but it will return to its original shape when it is heated. It has **shape memory**. Many new uses are still being developed for this type of alloy.

Rusting Conditions

The diagram opposite shows an investigation into what conditions are needed to make a nail rust. Four nails were placed in test tubes in different conditions and left for a week. The only one that rusted was the nail in the third test tube. From this we can tell that rusting needs iron, water and oxygen (air).

Rust flakes off the iron exposing more metal to corrode. Rusting happens even faster when the water is salty or is made from acid rain. Cars can rust. They are usually scrapped when this happens because it makes the metal weaker. Aluminium does not rust or corrode in air and water. Instead, it quickly forms a layer of aluminium oxide when it comes into contact with air. This layer stops any more air or water from coming into contact with the metal. This built-in protection will not flake off.

> **HT** Rusting is an example of an **oxidation reaction**. This is a reaction where oxygen is added to a substance. Oxygen is added to the iron in the presence of water.
>
> Iron **+** Oxygen **+** Water ⟶ Hydrated iron (III) oxide

Only iron and steel rust; other metals corrode. The table below gives descriptions of metals in different conditions. In your exam you may be asked to interpret information on the rate of corrosion of different metals. For example, you could state that aluminium is the least corroded metal because even in salty wet air, its appearance is the least changed (it has only dulled).

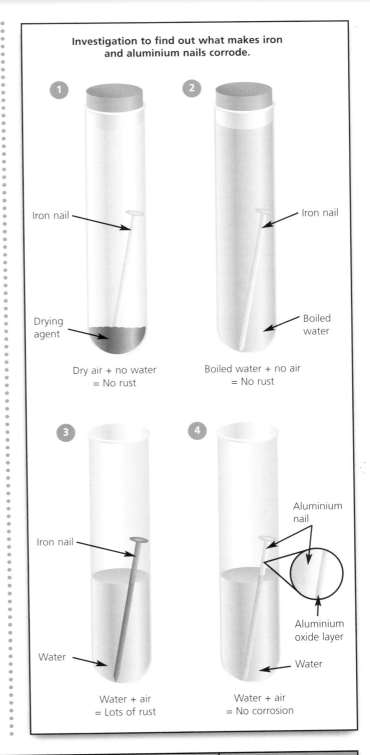

Investigation to find out what makes iron and aluminium nails corrode.

1. Iron nail — Drying agent — Dry air + no water = No rust
2. Iron nail — Boiled water — Boiled water + no air = No rust
3. Iron nail — Water — Water + air = Lots of rust
4. Aluminium nail — Aluminium oxide layer — Water — Water + air = No corrosion

Metal	Clean and Dry Air	Wet Air	Acidic Wet Air	Salty Wet Air
Steel	Shiny	Dull (rusty)	Very dull (rusty)	Very dull (rusty)
Copper	Shiny	Dull	Green layer	Green layer
Aluminium	Shiny	Shiny	Dull	Dull
Silver	Shiny	Shiny	Tarnished	Tarnished

Cars for Scrap

Properties of Metals

The table below shows the properties of aluminium and iron.

Property	Aluminium	Iron
Dense	✗	✔
Magnetic	✗	✔
Resists corrosion	✔	✗
Malleable	✔	✔
Conducts electricity	✔	✔

A car can be built using iron or aluminium as both metals can be pressed into shape; they are both malleable.

Aluminium is well-suited to the job because…
- it does not corrode (whereas iron does)
- it is less dense than iron (which means the car will be lighter).

However, iron is well-suited to the job because…
- it is cheaper than aluminium
- it is magnetic (aluminium is not) which means it can be separated for recycling more easily.

Most cars are made from steel. Steel is an alloy of iron and carbon. Steel has different properties from iron which make it more useful. It is harder and does not corrode as fast as iron.

Pure aluminium is not strong or hard enough to build a car. The aluminium can be mixed with metals such as copper and magnesium to create an alloy.

HT Some expensive cars are made from aluminium. Aluminium does not rust or corrode so the car will last for longer. And because aluminium is less dense than steel the car will…
- be lighter
- need less fuel
- have better performance.

Materials in a Car

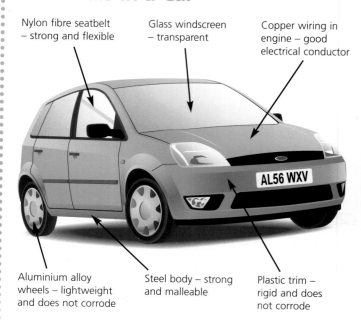

Nylon fibre seatbelt – strong and flexible

Glass windscreen – transparent

Copper wiring in engine – good electrical conductor

Aluminium alloy wheels – lightweight and does not corrode

Steel body – strong and malleable

Plastic trim – rigid and does not corrode

AL56 WXV

Recycling

Most materials used in a car can be recycled. From 2006, the law requires that 85% of a car must be recycled; this will increase to 95% in 2015.

The problem is separating all the different materials from each other. However, there are many benefits. Recycling materials means…
- less quarrying
- less energy used in their extraction from ores
- the limited ore reserves will last longer.

Recycling the plastics and fibres reduces the amount of crude oil needed to make them and conserves oil reserves. There are a number of materials in a car that would cause pollution if put into landfill, e.g. lead in the car battery. Recycling protects the environment.

HT Look at the diagram of the car above, for each material you should be able to list the properties and explain why it has been used. For example…
- windscreen glass is transparent and shatterproof
- plastic trim does not corrode, it is easy to shape and is rigid.

The Changing Atmosphere

The Earth's atmosphere has not always been the same as it is today. It has gradually evolved over billions of years.

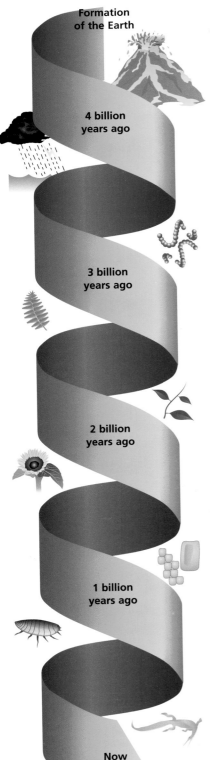

Formation of the Earth

The earliest atmosphere contained ammonia and carbon dioxide. These gases came from inside the Earth and were often released through the action of volcanoes.

4 billion years ago

As the temperature of the planet fell, the water vapour in the atmosphere condensed to form the oceans and seas.

3 billion years ago

The evolution of plants meant that photosynthesis started to reduce the amount of carbon dioxide and increase the amount of oxygen in the atmosphere.

2 billion years ago

1 billion years ago

Now

Clean air contains about 78% nitrogen, 21% oxygen, and 1% other gases, including 0.035% carbon dioxide. It also contains varying amounts of water vapour and some polluting gases.

Respiration and Photosynthesis

All living things respire. They use oxygen to release energy from food and give out carbon dioxide. This decreases the oxygen levels and increases the carbon dioxide levels in the air.

Animals respire all the time, plants respire only at night. During the day, plants photosynthesise. This is the opposite of respiration: they take in carbon dioxide and release oxygen. This balances out and so the levels of carbon dioxide and oxygen in the air remain fairly constant.

Theories of Atmospheric Change

Explanations about how our planet and its atmosphere have evolved are scientists' best efforts at interpreting all the available evidence. Below is one suggested explanation. But remember, it is only a theory!

A hot volcanic Earth would have released various gases into the atmosphere, just as volcanoes do nowadays. These gases would probably have included water vapour, carbon dioxide (and small amounts of ammonia, methane and sulfur dioxide).

As the Earth cooled down, its surface temperature would have gradually fallen below 100°C and water vapour would have condensed.

The oxygen level in the atmosphere is maintained by photosynthesis in green plants. We must assume that the atmosphere contained oxygen when organisms that could carry out photosynthesis first appeared.

Nitrifying bacteria use up ammonia from their surroundings and convert it into nitrates. These in turn are converted into unreactive nitrogen. It is unlikely, therefore, that these processes removed ammonia from the earlier atmosphere and produced the nitrogen gas which makes up 78% of air today.

Clean Air

Air Pollution

In
- Air – mostly nitrogen and oxygen.
- Hydrocarbon fuel such as petrol or diesel.

Out
- The normal products of combustion.
- **Carbon monoxide** – poisonous gas made when the fuel does not burn completely.
- **Oxides of nitrogen** – the spark inside the engine causes the nitrogen and oxygen in the air to react.

Pollutant gases are formed from…
- the burning of fossil fuels
- incomplete combustion in a car engine.

The table below includes information on how pollutant gases are produced, and what environmental problems they lead to. In your exam you may be asked to use information such as this to make judgements about the effects of air pollution, e.g. how it affects people's health.

Activity	Gas produced
Car exhausts	• Carbon monoxide (poisonous). • Nitrogen dioxide (leads to acid rain). • Unburned hydrocarbons (creates smog).
Coal fires	• Sulfur dioxide (leads to acid rain).
Burning fuels	• Carbon dioxide (leads to global warming).
Aerosols	• CFCs (damage the ozone layer).

Burning fossil fuels (which are all carbon compounds) increases the amount of carbon dioxide in the atmosphere. However, this carbon dioxide can be used for photosynthesis.

It is important to reduce air pollution as much as possible because it can damage our surroundings and can adversely affect people's health. One way to remove carbon dioxide from car exhausts is to fit a **catalytic converter**. The catalyst makes the carbon monoxide react to make carbon dioxide.

Acid Rain

When coal or oils are burned, the sulfur impurities produce sulfur dioxide. Sulfur dioxide (and nitrogen dioxide) gas dissolves in water to produce acid rain. Acid rain can…
- damage trees, erode stonework and corrode metals
- make rivers and lakes acidic
- kill plants.

HT Human Influence on the Atmosphere

Until relatively recently, the balance between adding and removing carbon dioxide from the atmosphere has remained constant. The levels of carbon dioxide and oxygen were maintained by photosynthesis and respiration. However, three important factors have upset the balance.

1 Excessive burning of fossil fuels is increasing the amount of carbon dioxide in the atmosphere.

2 Deforestation on large areas of the Earth's surface means the amount of photosynthesis is reduced so less carbon dioxide is removed from the atmosphere.

3 Increase in world population has directly and indirectly contributed to 1 and 2.

In addition to these problems, the atmosphere is becoming steadily more polluted with sulfur dioxide and unburned hydrocarbons.

To help reduce the amount of pollutants being put into the atmosphere, catalytic converters are fitted to cars to convert the carbon monoxide in exhaust gases to the less harmful carbon dioxide.

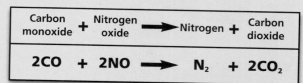

Faster or Slower (1)

There are four important factors which affect the rate of reaction…

- **temperature** (see below)
- **concentration** (see below)
- **surface area** (see p.88)
- use of a **catalyst** (see p.88).

Temperature of the Reactants

Low Temperature	High Temperature
In a cold reaction mixture, the particles are moving quite slowly. The particles will collide with each other less often, with less energy, so fewer collisions will be successful.	If the temperature of the reaction mixture is increased, the particles will move faster. They will collide with each other more often, with greater energy, so many more collisions will be successful.

Concentration of the Reactants

Low Concentration	High Concentration
In a reaction where one or both reactants are in low concentrations, the particles are spread out. The particles will collide with each other less often, resulting in fewer successful collisions.	Where there are high concentrations of one or both reactants, the particles are crowded close together. The particles will collide with each other more often, resulting in many more successful collisions.

Pressure of a Gas

Low Concentration	High Concentration
When a gas is under a low pressure, the particles are spread out. The particles will collide with each other less often resulting in fewer successful collisions. (This is like low concentration of liquid reactants.)	When the pressure is high, the particles are crowded more closely together. The particles collide more often, resulting in many more successful collisions. (This is like high concentration of liquid reactants.)

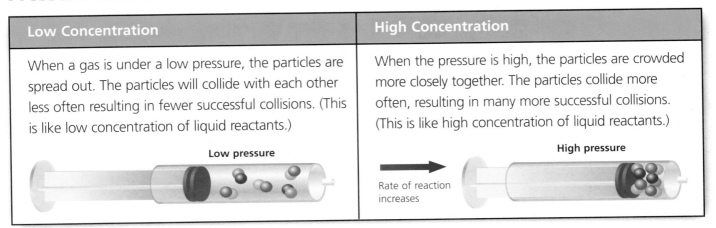

Low pressure　　　Rate of reaction increases　　　**High pressure**

Faster or Slower (1)

Collision Theory

Chemical reactions only occur when reacting **particles collide** with each other with sufficient **energy** to react. These reactions can proceed at different speeds.

- Rusting is a slow reaction.
- Burning is a fast reaction.
- An explosion is a fast reaction.

Increasing **temperature** causes an increase in the kinetic energy of the particles, i.e. they move a lot faster. The faster the particles move the greater the chance of them colliding, so the number of collisions per second increases. The more collisions there are between particles, the faster the reaction.

When the particles collide at an increased temperature they have more energy. When the collision has more energy, the chance of it causing a successful collision is increased (energetic collisions = more successful collisions).

Increasing **concentration** increases the number of particles in the same space, i.e. the particles are much more crowded together.

The more crowded the particles are, the greater the chance of them colliding together, which increases the number of collisions per second. (More frequent collisions not just more collisions.)

HT More on Collision Theory

The rate of reaction depends on...
- how frequently the particles collide – the more collisions the more chance of a successful or effective collision, which increases the rate of reaction
- the amount of energy transferred during the collision – the more energy transferred in a collision, the more chance of the collision being successful or effective, which increases the rate of reaction.

Measuring the Rate of Reaction

Chemical reactions stop when one of the reactants is used up. We can calculate the rate of a chemical reaction in two ways...
- calculating (measuring) the rate at which reactants are used up (see ① below)
- calculating (measuring) the rate at which products are formed (see ② below).

Example

① Measure the mass of the reaction mixture. If a gas is produced, the mass of the reaction mixture will decrease.

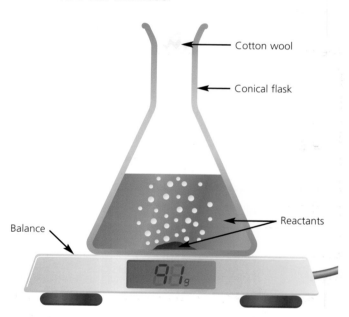

② Measure the volume of gas produced.

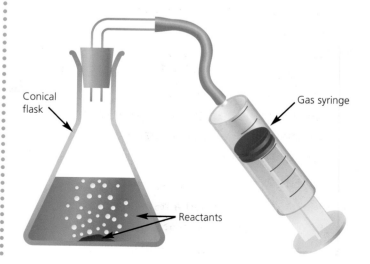

Analysing the Rate of Reaction

Two chemical reactions were carried out and the following results were obtained.

Time (s)	Volume of A (ml)	Volume of B (ml)
0	0	0
30	22	18
60	40	35
90	54	49
150	62	57
180	62	62

These results can be sketched on a graph to show the progress of the chemical reactions.

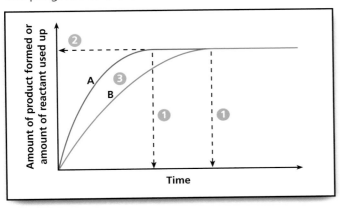

We can use the graph to find out…

1 **how long it takes to make the products**. The flat line on the graph indicates that the reaction is finished and that the products have been made. By drawing a vertical line down to the x-axis (time) from the flat line we can see how long this took

2 **how much product was made** by drawing a horizontal line from the highest point on the graph across to the y-axis

3 **which reaction is quicker** by comparing the steepness of the lines (the steeper the line the quicker the reaction).

By comparing the reactions, we can conclude that reaction A could have had a more concentrated reactant than reaction B, or the reaction could have been carried out at a higher temperature.

Another two chemical reactions were carried out. This time, the temperature and the concentration of the reactants were the same but less reactant was used in reaction B. As you can see from the graph below, the reaction happens in the same time but less product is formed.

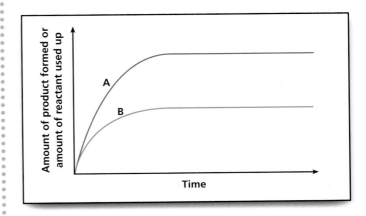

⒣ Further Use of Graphs

The points used to plot the graph are shown as crosses.

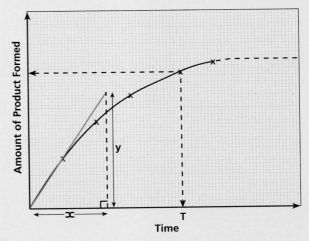

We can now do these additional things:
- calculate the initial rate of reaction by drawing a straight line following the start of the curve and working out $\frac{y}{x}$
- extend the curve by estimating the most likely path it will take next.
- work out the amount of product formed by a time (T) for which we did not have a reading.

Faster or Slower (2)

Surface Area of Solid Reactants

The larger the surface area of a reactant in relation to its volume, the faster the reaction. Powdered solids have the largest surface area and can therefore have very fast reactions; much faster than a lump of the same reactant. This is because there are more particles available on the surface for the other reactants to collide with. The greater the number of particles exposed, the greater the chance of them colliding together, which increases the reaction. (More collisions = faster reaction.)

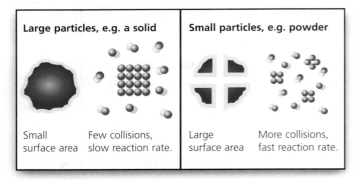

Large particles, e.g. a solid	Small particles, e.g. powder
Small surface area Few collisions, slow reaction rate.	Large surface area More collisions, fast reaction rate.

Factories that handle powders such as flour, custard powder or sulfur have to be very careful because the dust of these materials can mix with air and could cause an explosion if there is a spark. (An explosion is a very fast reaction where huge volumes of gas are made.) The factories have to prevent dust being produced and take precautions to ensure no spark is made that would ignite a dust/air mixture. Other materials that explode are hydrogen, TNT and dynamite.

Using a Catalyst

A catalyst is a substance that increases the rate of a chemical reaction without being changed during the process. Catalysts are very useful materials, as only a small amount of catalyst is needed to speed up the reaction of large amounts of reactant.

Consider the decomposition of hydrogen peroxide…

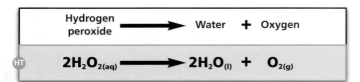

Hydrogen peroxide → Water + Oxygen

HT $2H_2O_{2(aq)} \longrightarrow 2H_2O_{(l)} + O_{2(g)}$

We can measure the rate of this reaction by measuring the amount of oxygen given off at one minute intervals. This reaction happens very slowly unless we add a catalyst of manganese (IV) oxide. With a catalyst, plenty of fizzing can be seen as the oxygen is given off at a faster rate.

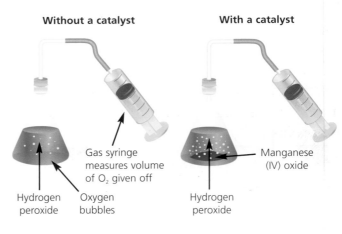

Without a catalyst   **With a catalyst**

Gas syringe measures volume of O_2 given off

Hydrogen peroxide   Oxygen bubbles   Hydrogen peroxide   Manganese (IV) oxide

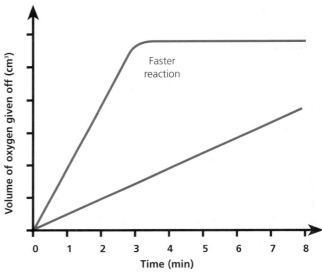

Faster reaction

(graph: Volume of oxygen given off (cm³) vs Time (min), 0–8)

HT Catalysts are specific to certain reactions: a catalyst for one reaction will not work for another.

Catalysts (like reactants) are most effective when they have a large surface area. The greater the number of particles exposed, the greater the chance of them colliding together, which means the number of collisions per second increases. (More frequent collisions, not just more collisions.)

Collecting Energy from the Sun

Photocells

A **photocell** has a flat surface made of silicon which captures as much of the light energy from the Sun as possible. It transfers this light energy into an electric current which travels in the same direction all the time (direct current, DC).

The power output of the photocells depends on the area exposed to the sunlight, so lots of photocells can be joined together to create a larger surface and therefore increase the amount of light captured from the Sun. A collection of photocells is called a **solar panel**.

The advantages and disadvantages of photocells are listed alongside.

Advantages

- Robust and require little maintenance once installed.
- Can operate in remote locations to give access to electricity without installing power cables.
- No need for fuel because the Sun is the source of energy.
- Have a long life.
- Use energy from the Sun which is a renewable energy source.
- No pollution or waste produced.

Disadvantages

- Expensive to buy.
- No power at night or during bad weather.

How Photocells Work

The Sun's energy is absorbed by the photocell, causing **electrons** to be knocked loose from the silicon crystal. These electrons flow freely within the silicon. This flow of charge is called an **electric current**.

The power of a photocell depends on the surface area exposed to the light and the **intensity** of that light. (Intensity is a measure of how concentrated the light energy is.)

To maximise power output, an efficient solar collector must track (follow) the position of the Sun in the sky. This requires technology which increases the initial setup cost.

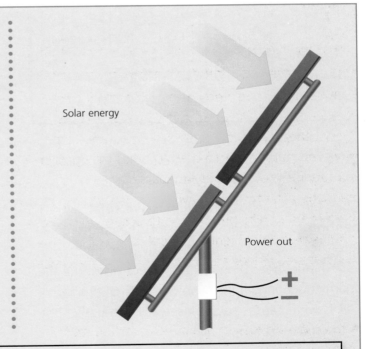

Solar energy

Power out

+
−

The solar panel moves to track the Sun's position

Collecting Energy from the Sun

Harnessing the Sun's Energy

Light from the Sun can be captured and used in other ways too.

Light can be **absorbed** by a surface and transferred into heat energy. Water passed over this surface will be heated to a reasonable temperature and can be used for heating buildings.

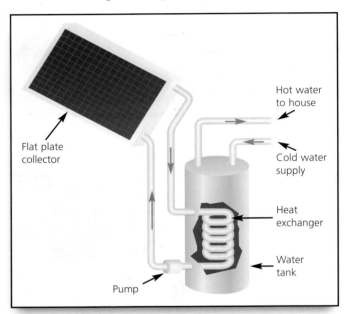

A **curved mirror** can be used to focus the Sun's light, rather like a magnifying glass.

Glass can be used to provide **passive solar heating** for buildings. Passive solar heating simply refers to a device that traps energy from the Sun (e.g. a greenhouse) but that does not distribute the energy or change it into another form of energy. This is what causes your conservatory to get so hot in the summer.

More on Passive Solar Heating

Glass is transparent to **visible light** so it passes straight through it, into our homes where it is absorbed by the objects in the room.

The heated surfaces then emit **infrared** light, which is reflected back into the room by the glass.

Wind Turbines

Wind turbines depend upon the convection currents in the air (wind) produced by the Sun's energy. Wind turbines transfer the **kinetic energy** of the air into **electrical energy**.

Wind turbines

Wind Turbines

The advantages and disadvantages of wind turbines are listed below.

Advantages
• Wind is a **renewable** energy source so will not run out.
• There is no chemical **pollution** or **waste**.
• Turbines are sturdy and strong.

Disadvantages
• Require a large amount of **space** to deliver a reasonable amount of electricity.
• **Dependent** on the wind.
• Cause **visual pollution** because they are very big.

Generating Electricity

The Dynamo Effect

Electricity can be generated by moving a wire, or a coil of wire, near a magnet or vice versa. When this happens the wire cuts through the lines of force of the magnetic field and a current is produced in the wire, providing it is part of a complete circuit.

Electricity can be generated by moving the magnet towards the coil of wire.

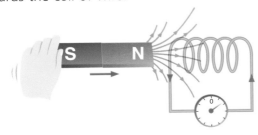

Or by moving the coil of wire towards the magnet.

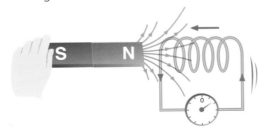

The current generated can be increased by…

• using stronger magnets
• using more turns in the coil
• moving the coil (or magnet) faster.

Generators use this principle to produce electricity. Batteries produce a direct current but generators produce an **alternating current** (AC). This means that the direction of the current is continually alternating as time passes.

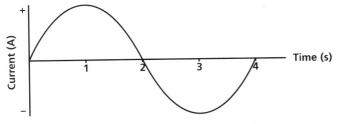

The graph shows that as time passes, the line curves up and down again. The current alternates from a positive direction to a negative one and back again.

HT The **frequency** of AC electricity is the number of cycles that are completed every second. In the graph, it takes 4 seconds for one cycle so the frequency is 0.25 cycles per second.

The AC Generator

In an AC generator, a coil of wire is rotated in a magnetic field. In practice, the coil and field should be close together. As the coil cuts through the magnetic field a current is generated in the coil. The current alternates, i.e. it reverses its direction of flow every half turn of the coil, as can be seen below…

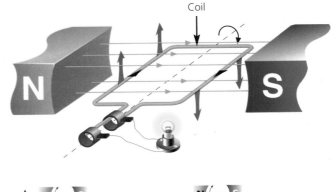

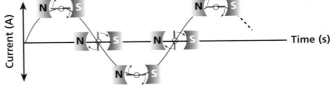

Producing Electricity

The heat energy for our power stations comes from a variety of fuels. The fuel is burnt to release heat energy which boils water to produce steam which drives the turbines and, ultimately, the generators which produce electricity.

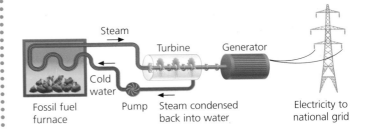

Power Station (1)

Fuels for Power

The type of fuel we use depends upon the economical and environmental costs. Common fuels used are…

- **fossil fuels** – crude oil, coal and natural gas (burning fuels releases energy in the form of heat)
- **renewable biomass** – wood, straw and manure (biomass can be fermented to generate **methane gas**)
- **nuclear fuel** (uranium fuel rods release energy as heat).

Nuclear Power

Nuclear power stations use **uranium** fuel rods to release energy as heat. Uranium, like coal, is a non-renewable resource so will run out one day. Although nuclear power does not contribute to global warming, the **waste** is **radioactive** and can be harmful because it has ionising radiations that can cause **cancer**. One of the waste products from nuclear reactors is **plutonium** which can be used to make nuclear bombs.

Distributing Electricity

Electricity generated at power stations is distributed to homes, offices, farms, factories, etc. all over the country by a network of power lines called the National Grid. Transformers are used to step up and step down the voltage before and after transmission. The electricity is transmitted through power lines at high voltage to **reduce energy waste** and costs.

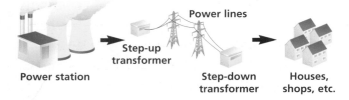

Power lines

Step-up transformer

Step-down transformer

Power station

Houses, shops, etc.

HT If you send a large current through a power cable it will soon become very hot and much of the electrical energy will be lost to heat energy. Transformers step up the voltage to reduce the current, which reduces energy loss due to heating.

Efficiency of a Power Station

A significant amount of energy produced by conventional power stations is wasted. At each stage in the electricity transfer process, energy is transferred to the surroundings in a 'non-useful' form, usually as heat. Below is a typical energy transfer diagram for the process that shows how much energy is wasted at each stage. Only 30J are used usefully, 70J are wasted.

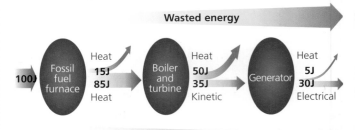

Wasted energy

	Heat		Heat		Heat
Fossil fuel furnace	15J	Boiler and turbine	50J	Generator	5J
100J	85J		35J		30J
	Heat		Kinetic		Electrical

Useful energy

HT The following equations are used when calculating the efficiency of a power station…

| Fuel energy input (J) | $=$ | Waste energy output (J) | $+$ | Electrical energy output (J) |

$$\text{Efficiency} = \frac{\text{Electrical energy output (J)}}{\text{Fuel energy input (J)}}$$

Example

A power station uses 200 000J of fuel energy to produce 80 000J of electrical energy.

a) What is the waste energy output?

Rearrange the first formula…

Waste energy output $=$ Fuel energy input $-$ Electrical energy output

$= 200\,000 - 80\,000$

$= \mathbf{120\,000J}$

b) What is the efficiency of this power station?

$$\text{Efficiency} = \frac{\text{Electrical energy output}}{\text{Fuel energy input}}$$

$$= \frac{80\,000}{200\,000}$$

$= 0.4 \times 100$ ◄ Multiply by 100 to get a percentage

$= \mathbf{40\%}$

Comparing Fuel and Energy Sources

The table below lists the advantages and disadvantages of different types of fuel and renewable energy sources.

Source	Advantages	Disadvantages
Fossil fuel, e.g. coal, oil, gas	• Enough reserves for short to medium term. • Relatively cheap and easy to obtain. • Coal-, oil- and gas-fired power stations are flexible in meeting demand and have a relatively quick start-up time. • Burning gas doesn't produce SO_2.	• Produces CO_2 which causes acid rain and SO_2 (except burning gas) which causes global warming. • Removing SO_2 from waste gases to reduce global warming adds to the cost. • Oil is often carried between continents in tankers, leading to risk of spillage and pollution. • Expensive pipelines and networks are often required to transport it to the point of use.
Biomass, e.g. wood, straw, manure	• It is renewable. • Can be burned to produce heat. • Burned manure produces methane.	• Produces CO_2 and SO_2 which damage the environment. • Large area needed to grow trees which could be used for other purposes, e.g. growing food.
Nuclear fuel, e.g. uranium	• Cost and rate of fuel is relatively low. • Can be situated in sparsely populated areas. • Nuclear power stations are flexible in meeting demand. • Does not produce CO_2 or SO_2 (greenhouse gases). • High stocks of nuclear fuel. • Can reduce use of fossil fuels.	• Radioactive material can stay dangerously radioactive for thousands of years and can be harmful. • Storing radioactive waste is very expensive. • Building and decommissioning nuclear power stations are costly. • Comparatively long start-up time. • Radioactive material could be emitted. • Pollution from fuel processing. • High maintenance costs.
Renewable sources, e.g. wind, tidal, hydro-electric, solar	• No fuel costs during operation. • No chemical pollution. • Often low maintenance. • Do not contribute to global warming or produce acid rain. • Produces free, clean electricity. • Can be constructed in remote areas.	• With the exception of hydroelectric, they produce small amounts of electricity. • Take up lots of space and are unsightly. • Unreliable (apart from hydroelectric), depend on the weather and cannot guarantee supply on demand. • High initial capital outlay.

Power Station (2)

Measuring Electricity Use

Your electricity meter at home will look similar to the one shown above. It will show a count of units. These units represent kilowatt hours (kWh), which are a measure of how much electricity has been used.

Kilowatt Hours

The number of kWh units of electricity used by an appliance depends on…

- the power rating in kilowatts (kW) of the appliance
- the time in hours (h) the appliance is switched on for.

To calculate the number of kWh (units) used and the cost of units used, we need to use the following formulae…

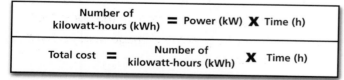

Example

A 1.5kW electric hot plate was switched on for 2 hours. How much does the electricity used cost if electricity is 8p per kWh?

First, calculate the number of kilowatt hours used, using the formula…

Number of kWh = Power x Time

= 1.5kW x 2h

= 3kWh

Then, calculate the cost…

Total cost = Number of kWh used x Cost per unit

= 3 x 8

= 24p

Measuring Energy Supplied

The kilowatt hour is a measure of how much electricity has been used. It is also a measure of how much electrical energy has been supplied. The above relationship can be written as…

$$\text{Energy supplied (kWh)} = \text{Power (kW)} \times \text{Time (h)}$$

$$\frac{E}{P \times t}$$

Example 1

A 200W CD player is used for 90 minutes. Calculate the energy supplied.

Using the formula…

Energy supplied = Power x Time

= 0.2kW x 1.5h

= 0.3kWh

> Power must be in kW and time must be in h.

Example 2

On a building site, 2.25kWh of electrical energy is supplied to an electric drill in 3 hours. What is the power rating of the electric drill?

Rearrange the formula…

$$\text{Power} = \frac{\text{Energy supplied}}{\text{Time}}$$

$$= \frac{2.25\text{kWh}}{3\text{h}}$$

= 0.75kW or 750W

N.B. To do these calculations, you must always remember to make sure the power is in kilowatts, and the time is in hours.

Power and Energy Transfer in Circuits

An electric current involves a flow of electric charge which transfers energy from the battery or power supply to the components in the circuit. If the component is a filament lamp, as in the circuit below, then most of the electrical energy is transformed into light.

The rate of this energy transfer determines the power of the component or device and is measured in joules/second or watts (W), where 1 watt is the transfer of 1 joule of energy in 1 second.

Power is calculated using the following relationship…

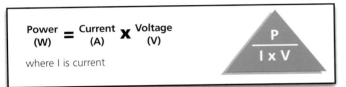

Power = Current x Voltage
(W)   (A)   (V)

where I is current

$\dfrac{P}{I \times V}$

Example

Calculate the power of the lamp below when the current flowing through it is 0.3A and the voltage across it is 3V.

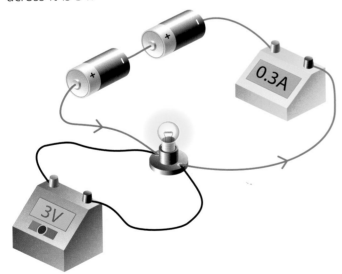

Using the formula…

Power = Current x Voltage

= 0.3A x 3V

= **0.9 watts**

This means that the lamp above transfers 0.9 joules of electrical energy in every second it is switched on.

Example

Calculate the current flowing through the iron (below) when it is being used at its maximum power and working voltage.

Power   Voltage

900W   230V-50Hz
WELLMAN
SUPERSTEAM
SERIAL No 6161623PW

Domestic iron rating plate

Rearranging the formula:

$$\text{Current} = \frac{\text{Power}}{\text{Voltage}}$$

$$= \frac{900W}{230V}$$

= **3.9 amps**

Off-peak Electricity

Electricity is supplied to our homes 24 hours a day. It is the favoured source of energy because no smoke or gases are produced in the home.

However, the electricity is generated using fossil fuels which produce pollution so the consumer is indirectly adding to the damage being caused to the environment.

Most electricity is used when people are awake and active. There is obviously less demand during the night when most people are asleep. In order to encourage people to use electricity during this quiet period, electricity boards offer cheaper electricity for seven hours every night, called **Economy-7**. It is used mainly for…

- heating up water and storage heaters
- powering washing machines and dishwashers.

For the consumer, the main advantage is cost since it is cheaper. But it is an inconvenience running washing machines during the night because they can be noisy.

Nuclear Radiations

Types of Radiation

Radioactive materials are substances that give out nuclear radiation all the time, regardless of what is done to them. Radioactivity involves a change in the structure of the radioactive atom and the release of one of the three types of nuclear radiation:

- alpha (α)
- beta (β)
- gamma (γ).

Unstable nucleus   New nucleus   α particle

Radiation that occurs naturally all around us is called **background radiation**. It only provides a very small dose altogether, so there is no danger to our health. Some sources of background radiation are radioactive substances in rocks and soil, and cosmic rays from outer space and the Sun.

Structure and Penetration

Each type of radiation has a different structure:

- alpha radiation is a **helium nucleus** which consists of two protons and two neutrons
- beta radiation is a fast moving **electron**
- gamma is very high frequency electromagnetic **radiation**.

The diagram below shows each type of radiation's penetrative power, i.e. what materials they can pass through.

Handling Radioactive Materials

There are four main **safety measures** that people who handle radioactive materials need to take:

- wear protective clothing
- keep your distance – use tongs to hold the material whenever possible
- try to minimise your exposure time
- store radioactive materials in clearly labelled, shielded containers so others are aware of what they are handling.

Some radioactive waste can be reprocessed but often it has to be disposed of. Low-level waste is sealed and buried in land-fill sites but higher level waste is mixed with sugar, bonded with glass, poured into a steel cylinder and kept underground.

HT The diagram below clearly shows that alpha, beta and gamma radiation all have different penetrating powers. We can use their penetrating powers to identify them.

There are four main problems to bear in mind when dealing with radioactive waste:

- it remains radioactive for a long time and we do not know how to dispose of it safely
- it may be a target for terrorist activity
- it needs to be kept out of ground water to avoid contaminating drinking supplies
- acceptable radioactivity levels may change over time so measures may need modifying.

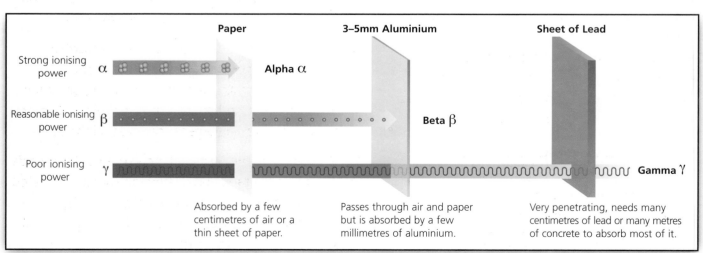

Strong ionising power   α   **Alpha α**

Reasonable ionising power   β   **Beta β**

Poor ionising power   γ   **Gamma γ**

Paper   3–5mm Aluminium   Sheet of Lead

Absorbed by a few centimetres of air or a thin sheet of paper.

Passes through air and paper but is absorbed by a few millimetres of aluminium.

Very penetrating, needs many centimetres of lead or many metres of concrete to absorb most of it.

Harmful Effects – Ionisation

If radiation particles collide with atoms, electrons may be knocked out of or into their structures. This losing or gaining of electrons alters their structure and leaves them as charged particles called **ions**.

Alpha, beta and gamma radiation are therefore known as **ionising radiation**. They can ionise materials and damage 'healthy' molecules in living cells, which results in the death of the cell. This can also lead to cancer.

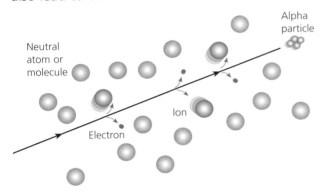

N.B. Ionisation can be explained as either the removal of electrons from particles or the gain of electrons by particles. In both cases we end up with ions (charged particles).

Use of Alpha Radiation

Most smoke detectors contain americium-241, which emits alpha radiation.

The emitted alpha particles cause the ionisation of air particles and the ions formed are attracted to the oppositely charged electrodes. This results in a current flowing in the circuit. When smoke enters the space between the two electrodes, less ionisation takes place as the alpha particles are absorbed by the smoke particles. A smaller current then flows, and the alarm sounds.

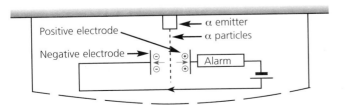

Uses of Beta Radiation

A **tracer** is a small amount of a radioactive substance which is put into a system so that its progress through the system can be followed using a radiation detector. A beta emitter tracer can be used to…
- detect tumours in certain parts of a patient's body, e.g. brain, lungs
- identify plants that have been fed with a fertiliser containing beta particles. (This method can be used to develop better fertilisers.)

When beta radiation passes through paper, some of it is absorbed. The greater the thickness of the paper, the greater the absorption. This idea can be used in a **paper thickness gauge**. If the paper thickness is too great, then more beta radiation is absorbed, and less passes through to the detector. A signal is then sent to the rollers to move closer which reduces the thickness of the paper.

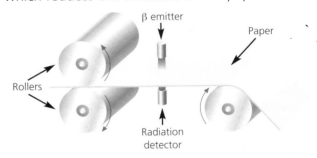

Uses of Gamma Radiation

Gamma radiation can be used to **treat cancer** because it destroys cancerous cells. A high, calculated dose is used from different angles so that only cancerous cells are destroyed and not the healthy cells.

Gamma radiation can also be used to **sterilise medical equipment** because it can destroy microorganisms like bacteria. An advantage of this method is that no heat is required, which minimises the damage to equipment that heat might cause.

Non-destructive tests can be carried out on welds using gamma radiation. A gamma source is situated on one side and any crack or defects can be identified using a detector (e.g. photographic film) situated on the other side.

Our Magnetic Field

The Earth's Magnetic Field

The Earth has a magnetic field around it which, just like a magnet, has a north pole and a south pole which can be detected using a plotting compass.

Although no one is certain what causes this field, it may be due to electric currents generated in the Earth's core which contains a lot of **molten iron**.

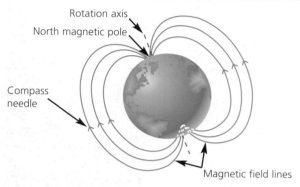

All charged particles are deflected by magnetic fields and the Earth's magnetic field protects us from charged **cosmic rays**. These rays are **ionising radiation** from the rest of the Universe.

Solar Flares

Much of the ionising radiation we receive comes from the Sun. Solar flares are clouds of **charged particles** that are ejected at **high speed** from the Sun. These moving charged particles produce magnetic fields so solar flares produce very **strong, disturbed magnetic fields** that can interfere with the operation of **artificial satellites** that we use for…

- telecommunications, e.g. television, telephones, etc.
- forecasting the weather
- spying
- navigation systems, e.g. in cars, planes.

Magnetic Field around a Coil

When electric current (moving electrically charged particles) is passed through a coil, a magnetic field is created.

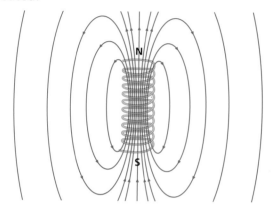

Notice that it looks just like the magnetic field around a bar magnet.

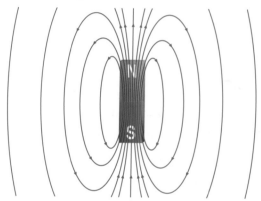

The Earth–Moon System

The magnetic field protecting the Earth may be the result of a gigantic collision in the past. The theory is that two planets collided and the iron cores of each planet then merged to form the Earth, and the less dense material formed the Moon which orbits the Earth.

Magnetic fields can be generated by a current (moving electrically charged particles).

Cosmic rays are fast moving particles which create **gamma** rays when they hit our atmosphere. The beautiful **Aurora Borealis** (or Northern Lights) is caused when cosmic rays spiral around the Earth's magnetic field towards the poles.

The consequences of a solar flare arriving at the Earth depend on its size but it can affect both **satellite communication** and **electricity distribution**.

The Universe

The Universe consists of…

- **stars**, one of which is our Sun. They can be clearly seen even though they are far away because they are very hot and give out light
- **planets**, **comets** and **meteors**
- **galaxies**, which are large groups of stars
- **black holes**, which are dense, dying stars with a strong gravitational field.

The Solar System

The **Solar System** is made up of the Sun (which is in the centre) surrounded by planets, comets and satellites. The nine planets (see diagram 1) move around the Sun in paths called **orbits** which are slightly squashed circles (ellipses). The planets, comets and satellites are kept in their orbits by the **gravitational force** of the larger body they are orbiting.

The Moon, Comets and Meteors

The Moon is in orbit around the Earth in the same way that the Earth is in orbit around the Sun.

Comets have a core of frozen gas and dust and they have an elliptical orbit around the Sun. They can be up to 20km in diameter. As they approach the Sun, the gases evaporate to form the tail, making the comet easy to see.

Meteors or shooting stars are fragments of dust and rock. They are much smaller than comets. As they enter the Earth's atmosphere they burn up due to friction and give out light which makes them easy to see.

HT The planets, comets and satellites travel in circular (or near circular) paths around a larger object. They stay in their orbits because the larger object exerts an **inward pull force** on them. This inward pull force is provided by **gravity** and is called the **centripetal force**, e.g. the Earth orbits the Sun because of its gravitational pull force.

The Sun and the planets in the Solar System

Sun
Mercury
Venus
Earth
Mars
Jupiter
Saturn
Uranus
Neptune
Pluto

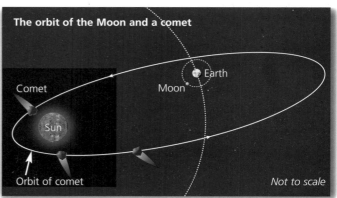

The orbit of the Moon and a comet

Comet
Sun
Earth
Moon
Orbit of comet

Not to scale

Exploring our Solar System

Manned Space Travel

Space is a very dangerous place. Some of the many difficulties which face a manned space mission to the planets, include…

- the planets are very, very far away so it takes months or even years to reach them
- the fuel required takes up most of the spacecraft
- room must be found to store enough food, water and oxygen for the whole journey
- a stable artificial atmosphere must be maintained in the spacecraft
- the temperature in space is freezing, so keeping warm is vitally important
- outside of the Earth's magnetic field, humans need shielding from cosmic rays
- the low gravity affects people's health
- radio signals would take a very long time to reach home!

Unmanned Space Travel

A far more realistic option is to explore our Solar System using unmanned spaceships. As well as being able to withstand conditions that are lethal to humans, these probes would not require food, water or oxygen.

Once arrived, probes could be used to send back information about the planet's…

- temperature
- magnetic field
- radiation levels
- gravity
- atmosphere
- surrounding landscape.

HT There are many advantages and disadvantages of using unmanned spacecraft to explore the Solar System.

Advantages

- **Costs** are lower as there is no need to provide space and provisions (food, water and oxygen) for human passengers.
- With no humans aboard, safety is no longer a consideration.

Disadvantages

- **Reliability** has to be high as there will be no-one to fix any breakdowns.
- Instruments must require zero **maintenance**.

Once the probe arrives on a planet, it can send information to Earth through radio waves which travel at the **speed of light**. The distance light travels in a year is called a **light year**. We use this measurement when talking about **very large distances**.

Asteroids

Asteroids are rocks left over from the formation of the Solar System. They normally orbit the Sun in a belt between Mars and Jupiter but occasionally they get knocked off course and head towards Earth.

When an asteroid collides with the Earth there can be several devastating consequences:

- the impact would form a crater, which could trigger the ejection of **hot rocks**
- the heat may cause widespread **fires**
- sunlight could be blocked out by the **dust** from the explosion
- **climate** change
- whole species could become **extinct**, which could affect other species.

There is good evidence to suggest that asteroids have collided with the Earth many times in the past:

- craters can be found all over the planet
- there are layers of unusual elements found in rocks
- there are abrupt changes in the number of fossils found in adjacent rock layers, which could be due to the sudden death of many animals.

> **HT** If asteroids in the belt of asteroids between Jupiter and Mars bump into each other they may join up or shatter, but Jupiter's strong gravitational pull prevents them from combining to form a planet.

Comets

A comet is a small body with a core of frozen gas and dust, which come from the objects orbiting the Sun far beyond the planets. Their characteristic tails are a trail of debris.

They have highly elliptical orbits around the Sun (our star). The speed of the comet increases as it approaches the Sun. This increased speed would make it even more dangerous in the event of an impact as it would have more energy.

> **HT** The comet's speed increases as a result of the increase in the strength of gravity as it approaches the star. It can also be affected by the gravity of planets.

Near Earth Objects (NEOs)

A Near Earth Object is an asteroid or comet on a possible **collision course** with Earth. **Telescopes** are used to observe these objects in an attempt to determine their **trajectories** (probable paths).

> **HT** NEOs may pose a threat to the human race but there are actions we can take to reduce that threat. We can…
> - **survey** the skies with telescopes to identify likely NEOs as early as possible
> - **monitor** their progress with satellites
> - **deflect** the object with an explosion if a collision does seem likely.

The Big Bang

One theory that has been used to explain the evolution of the Universe to its present state is the **Big Bang** theory which states that the whole Universe is **expanding** and that it all started billions of years ago, in one place with a huge explosion, i.e. a big bang.

When we look at the stars we observe that all the galaxies are moving away from us and that distant galaxies are moving away more quickly.

We also observe that **microwave radiation** is received from all parts of the Universe.

HT By tracking the movement of the galaxies, we can estimate the **age** and **starting point** of the Universe.

Evidence for the original 'big bang' explosion has been obtained by the detection of microwaves which were produced as a by-product of this historic event. These microwaves can be detected as interference on a poorly tuned television.

Evidence for the expansion has also been obtained by the measurement of **red shift**. If a source of light moves away from us, the wavelengths of the light in its spectrum are longer than if the source was not moving.

This effect is known as red shift because the wavelengths are shifted towards the red end of the spectrum.

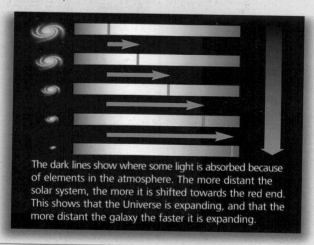

The dark lines show where some light is absorbed because of elements in the atmosphere. The more distant the solar system, the more it is shifted towards the red end. This shows that the Universe is expanding, and that the more distant the galaxy the faster it is expanding.

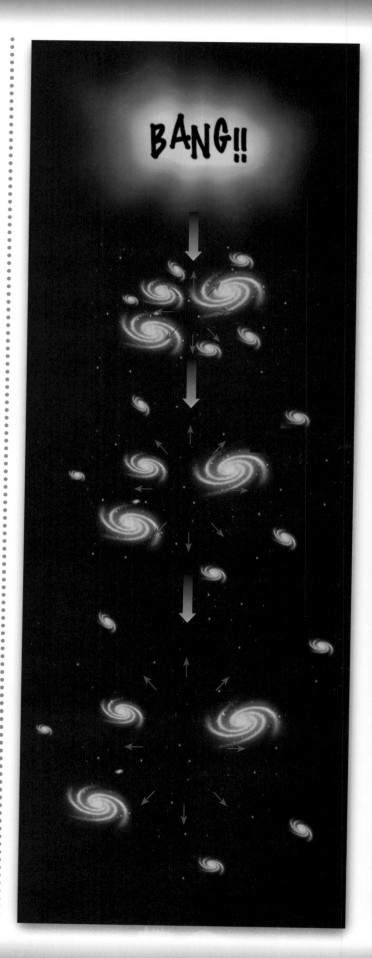

BANG!!

The End of a Star

All stars have a finite (limited) life. Eventually, the star's supply of hydrogen runs out and the star swells up becoming colder and colder to form a **red giant** or **red supergiant**.

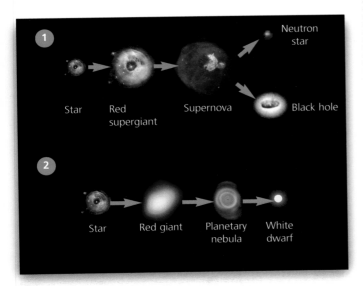

Stages for a Heavy Weight Star (see diagram 1)

Supernova – The red super giant rapidly shrinks and explodes releasing massive amounts of energy and dust and gas into space. This is a supernova.

Neutron star – For stars up to ten times the mass of our Sun the remnants of the supernova form a neutron star, formed only of neutrons. A cupful of this matter could have a mass greater than 15 000 million tonnes!

Black hole – Those stars greater than ten times the mass of our Sun are massive enough to leave behind black holes. Black holes can only be observed indirectly through their effects on their surroundings, e.g. the X-rays emitted when gases from a nearby star spiral into a black hole.

Stages for a Medium Weight Star (see diagram 2)

Planetary nebula – The core of the red giant contracts to be surrounded by outer shells of gas which eventually drift away into space.

White dwarf – As the core cools and contracts further it becomes a white dwarf with a density thousands of times greater than any matter on Earth.

HT Black holes can be found throughout the Universe and in every galaxy. They have a very **large mass** concentrated into a very small space which means that their **gravity** is very large. Not even light can escape from black holes.

The Formation of a Star

Stars, including our Sun, are formed when interstellar (between stars) gas clouds, which contain mainly hydrogen, collapse under gravitational attraction to form a proto-star.

Over a very long period of time the temperature of the proto-star increases as thermonuclear fusion reactions take place releasing massive amounts of energy and it finally becomes a main sequence star. During this time the forces of attraction pulling inwards are balanced by forces acting outwards and the star experiences a normal life. Eventually though the supply of hydrogen runs out causing the end of the star. The type of end depends largely on its mass.

Glossary

Adaptation – the gradual change of an organism over generations to better suit its environment

Aerobic respiration – respiration using oxygen which releases energy and produces CO_2 and water

Alloy – a mixture of two or more metals, or a metal and a non-metal

Anaerobic respiration – the incomplete breakdown of glucose without oxygen to produce a small amount of energy very quickly

Biodiversity – the variety of living organisms and ecosystems in which they live

Decompose – break down (thermal decomposition – breaking down by heating)

DNA – nucleic acid that contains the genetic information carried by every cell

Effector – the part of the body that responds to a stimulus

Electrolysis – the process by which an electric current causes a solution to undergo chemical decomposition

Evolve – to develop and change naturally over a period of time

Extinct – a species that has died out

Global warming – the gradual increase in the average temperature of the Earth

Greenhouse effect – the process by which the Earth is kept warm by the ozone reflecting heat back to the Earth

Hydrocarbon – a molecule containing only hydrogen and carbon atoms

Ion – a charged particle formed when an atom gains or loses an electron

Longitudinal wave – a wave that vibrates in the same direction as the wave travels, e.g. the type of wave produced by pushing a spring

Mutation – a change to the genetic code of a gene

Natural selection – a natural process resulting in the evolution of organisms well-adapted to the environment

Neurone – a specialised cell which transmits electrical messages or nerve impulses

Non-renewable resources – energy resources that cannot be replaced within a lifetime

Obesity – the condition of being very overweight

Pathogen – a disease-causing microorganism

Pollutants – chemicals that can harm the environment and organisms

Recycling – re-using materials that would otherwise be considered to be waste

Renewable resources – energy sources that can be replaced

Species – a group of organisms that can breed with each other to produce fertile offspring

Sustainable development – a policy to meet the needs of the present generation without compromising the ability of future generations to meet their own needs

Transverse wave – a wave (e.g. light) that vibrates at right angles to the direction of travel, i.e. has peaks and troughs

Acknowledgments

The authors and publisher would like to thank everyone who contributed images to this book:

IFC	©iStockphoto.com / Andrei Tchernov
p.4	©iStockphoto.com / Elio Gola
p.10	©iStockphoto.com / Matthew Cole
p.45	©iStockphoto.com / Stephen Sweet
p.45	©iStockphoto.com / Jolande Gerritsen
p.46	©iStockphoto.com / Kim Bryant
p.52	©iStockphoto.com / Luis Carlos Torres
p.53	©iStockphoto.com / Stephen Sweet
p.60	©iStockphoto.com / Dawn Hudson
p.74	©iStockphoto.com / Helle Bro Clemmensen
p.75	©iStockphoto.com / Luis Carlos Torres
p.94	©iStockphoto.com / Kim Bryant
p.99	©iStockphoto.com / George Argyropoulos
p.100	©iStockphoto.com / Stephen Sweet
p.101	©iStockphoto.com / Michael Knight

Artwork supplied by HL Studios